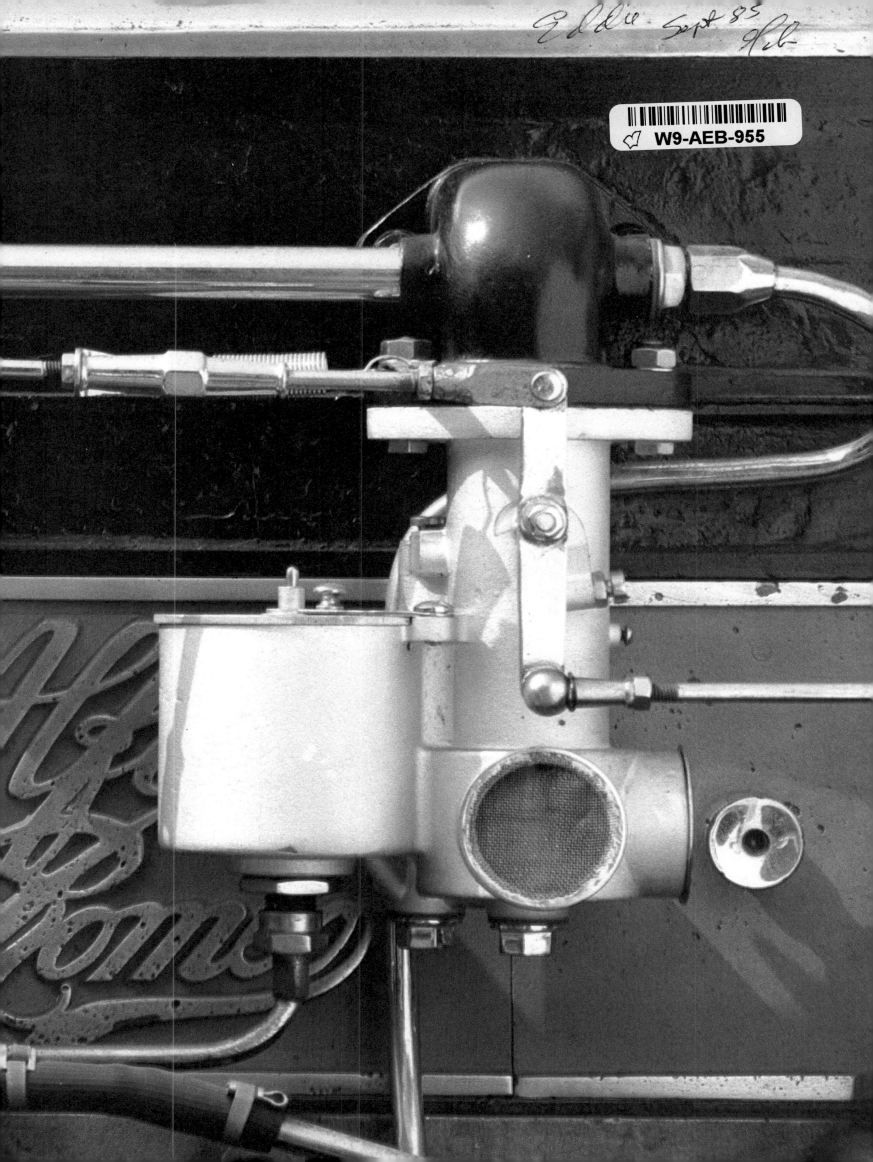

GREAT MARQUES

GREAT MARQUES

Alfa Romeo

David Owen

GENERAL EDITOR

John Blunsden

OCTOPUS BOOKS

Author's note

Any book like this depends on help and assistance from many people and organizations: but I should particularly like to thank the following: Neil Verweij, Ray Corsi and Domenico Magro of the Public Relations Department of Alfa Romeo SpA in Milan, for their ready co-operation in supplying the most detailed answers to every kind of question concerning the Alfas of today and yesterday. Likewise Barry Needham of Alfa Romeo (Great Britain) Ltd, without whom no book on Alfas could conceivably happen. Finally, my own store of information on Alfa history owes everything to Alvarez Garcia and Luigi Fusi, former guardians of the company archives and dedicated recorders of the mine of information which any writer on Alfa relies upon so completely.

David Owen

All cars unless otherwise stated in the captions were kindly provided by Alfa Romeo SpA or Alfa Romeo (Great Britain) Ltd. Owners and custodians of the other cars, at the time of writing, are mentioned in the captions to the illustrations.

Special photography in Italy and Great Britain by Ian Dawson

ENDPAPERS *Engine of the 1923 RL Targa Florio.*
PAGE 1 *1911 15 HP ALFA.* PAGES 2-3 *1938 8C 2900B Lungo.*
PAGES 4-5 *1967 1600 Spider Duetto, provided by Barry Coupe.*

**First published in 1985 by
Octopus Books Limited,
59 Grosvenor Street,
London W1**

© 1985 Octopus Books Limited

ISBN 0 7064 2219 8

Produced by Mandarin Publishers Limited,
22a Westlands Road, Quarry Bay,
Hong Kong

Printed in Hong Kong

CONTENTS

Modest Beginnings

Car history is inevitably full of surprises: many companies born with the best of pedigrees and the brightest of hopes end up all too soon in the commercial casualty ward. Either they close their doors under the pressure of bankruptcy, or they find themselves swallowed up by greedy and more successful rivals. All too soon the company name, and all it once stood for, dwindle to the size and significance of a different badge on an upmarket variant of a best-selling model, often with nothing at all in common with the designs that had created the company's original reputation.

Yet the opposite can still be true, even through the chaos and confusion of much of the 20th century. The fact remains that a company, which was first founded in 1906 as a simple commercial exercise to fulfil the demands of a poor and not very inviting market at minimum cost and maximum profit, is still very much alive and well – and independent, not part of a mammoth multinational. A company that was bankrupt within three years, renamed and re-formed twelve months later, taken over four years after that, rescued by government cash more than half a century ago and state-owned ever since. A company that has produced over the years some of the most advanced, most desirable, most agile and most beautiful of sports cars; a company that has done more for the sporting-saloon concept than any other manufacturer, that has won world championships in categories from sports cars to Grand Prix single-seaters. A company whose very name symbolizes the commercial threats and the narrow escapes of its fledgling years: Alfa Romeo of Milan.

Alfa's beginnings could hardly have been less promising. In the early 1900s, the Italian car market was considered hardly worth exploiting by the big manufacturers of France and Germany. Only Alexandre Darracq seemed to have the businessman's answer: to form an Italian-based subsidiary, using local labour to produce two of his older and smaller models under licence, at a cost low enough to make the whole project worth while. From an accountancy viewpoint, it was a well-planned operation.

Disaster — and revival

Commercially, however, the scheme was a disaster. Even by 1906, Italian buyers knew enough about motor cars to appreciate what the best of the European market could provide, and Darracq's Italian subsidiary, the Società Anonima Italiana Darracq (SAID), certainly was not delivering it. Because there was as yet no national motor industry, the Italians were having to import cars anyway: but if the home-grown car businesses could not match the best of the imports,

then there was no reason to buy their products. And Darracq's Italian-made cars could hardly have been less suited to Italian conditions. In a country where roads were often rough and gradients steep, the two SAID-made models, a single-cylinder 8/10 hp car and a 14 hp twin-cylinder design, were underpowered and temperamental, and sales were disappointing from the very beginning.

Within three years, Darracq himself – unwilling to upgrade the designs he entrusted to his Italian venture – was ready to cash in his investment. But fortunately for our story, there were others who had been involved in SAID who realized that, although the cars it had made were wrong, the basic idea was not. An ex-cavalry officer in the Italian army called Giovanni Agnelli had by now laid the foundations of the mighty Fiat empire, but there was still room for other car makers who could genuinely fill the needs of the Italian market. And Cavaliere Ugo Stella, SAID's Italian managing director, was one of those who could back up his beliefs with actions. In less than a year, Darracq had been paid off, production closed down, the company had been re-formed with just half the original share capital and an Italian car designer, Giuseppe Merosi, had been hired to produce some models that came closer to what people actually wanted to buy.

A new name — and a new hope

There was only one thing wrong. The name of SAID was now irretrievably linked with the old Darracq designs, which would blight the sales prospects of any new models the company produced. So from 24 June 1910 it had a new name – but not a grandiose or flamboyant one. Instead it was to soldier on with another set of initials, as the Anonima Lombarda Fabbrica Automobili ('Lombardy Car-Making Company'), or ALFA for short. The other half of the name was to come later.

Giuseppe Merosi had originally trained as a building surveyor, but he had gone on to make bicycles with a partner before designing cars and motorcycles and moving on to work for Fiat and Bianchi. He was a cautious man, and he knew full well that the most important attribute that would help his cars sell was reliability. On the punishing roads of the time, that meant simplicity and strength rather than performance: his cars would have to be solid and heavy, not light and fast.

All the same, Merosi's designs were a very long way ahead of the cumbersome Darracqs. He opted for four cylinders for the engines of both his original models, the four cylinders cast as a single block and head, bolted to a light alloy crankcase, which was forward thinking by the standards of the time. For the 24 HP, which was the first true Alfa, he specified a 100 mm cylinder bore and a stroke of 130 mm, which

PREVIOUS PAGES *The 40/60 was the largest of Merosi's designs for the fledgling ALFA company to appear before the First World War. This 1913 racing example, on a dirt road close to the company's test track at Balocco, typifies the car's size and toughness.*

LEFT *Giuseppe Merosi, although originally a surveyor by training, turned out a remarkably successful series of cars for ALFA in the critical early years of the company's existence. Here he sits at the wheel of one of his earliest creations, the ALFA 24 HP of 1910.*

ABOVE RIGHT *The Darracq connection gave birth to the company in 1906 – and nearly killed it off three years later with designs totally unsuited to the needs of the Italian market. This 8/10 HP made in 1908 was too underpowered to find many customers.*

produced a capacity of 4084 cc. This was a reasonably large engine, but it was given a tough job to do: the chassis he designed for the new car was a frame built up of two massive C-section steel girders running from the front of the car to the back, and curved where they passed over the rear axle. These were joined by a series of smaller cross members, set in between them like the rungs of a ladder. On top of this arrangement was an open tourer body on a wooden frame which could carry up to half a dozen passengers, and the wheels were suspended on simple but effective semi-elliptic leaf springs. Drum brakes were carried on the rear wheels, operated by a pedal and backed up by a hand lever for real emergencies.

Reliability first

This was a much bigger and more ambitious car than the tiny, underpowered Darracqs – the engine delivered four times the power of SAID's larger, twin-cylinder model – but at least it was reliable, thanks to a long and detailed testing programme Merosi arranged during the

latter months of 1910 before production began. Even though it turned the scales at more than a ton, the engine delivered enough power, channelled through a four-speed gearbox, to allow a top speed of 100 km/h (62 mph) and sales began slowly but assuredly to climb.

There was more on the way from the new company. Speed was still a luxury and a challenge on rough Italian roads, and Merosi had already decided to turn out a simpler, smaller and slower version of the 24 HP Alfa. This he achieved by narrowing the ladder frame by 25 mm (1 in) in width and shortening it by 230 mm (9 in) between the front and rear axles. It made the car smaller – just – than its predecessor, although the weight of the finished vehicle was just 90 kg (200 lb), or 10 per cent, lighter. It was slower because he designed a new version of the four-cylinder engine with narrower bores and a shorter stroke, which added up to a capacity of 2413 cc and a peak power output of 22 bhp. To make things worse, the engine was harnessed to a three-speed gearbox rather than the four-speed unit used on the 24 HP model. And in the circumstances the most amazing feature of the 15 HP, as the new Alfa

9

ALFA 24 HP			
Years made	1910–14		
No. made	300		

ENGINE		**DRIVE TRAIN**	
Type	In-line	Clutch	Multiple dry-plate
No. of cylinders	4	Transmission	4-speed gearbox
Bore/stroke mm	100 × 130		
Displacement cc	4084	**CHASSIS**	
Valve operation	Valves in inlet/exhaust tract operated by pushrods and springs from side-mounted camshaft	Frame	C-section girders in ladder frame
		Weight	1000 kg (2200 lb)
		Wheelbase	3200 mm (10 ft 6 in)
		Track	1450 mm (4 ft 9 in)
Sparkplugs per cyl.	1	Suspension	Semi-elliptic leaf springs
Compression ratio	4.15:1	Brakes	Drums on rear wheels
Induction	Single downdraught carburettor	Wheels	Artillery-type
BHP	45 at 2400 rpm	**PERFORMANCE**	
		Maximum speed	105 km/h (65 mph)

was called, was that its top speed only dropped to 89 km/h (55 mph), although it must have taken a great deal longer to reach this figure than its bigger stablemate.

Careful improvement and better prospects

Looked at dispassionately, Merosi's designs may appear dull and unenterprising. Yet in retrospect, there seems little doubt that he had his priorities right from the beginning. Road conditions were still verging on the primitive, and an extra few miles per hour in top speed came a long way behind reliability in most people's minds. What mattered was that the Alfas had the low-down torque to cope with hills, the braking power to come to a stop on poor surfaces, and the essential ruggedness to carry four or more passengers while still providing the driver with a car whose quality, if not its performance, he could feel enthusiastic about. There was little doubt that what mattered most at that stage was establishing a reputation for strength and endurance – the luxury of greater performance, when it came, would be a valuable and useful bonus.

Through the following years, Merosi's designs went on selling, steadily if unspectacularly – with detail improvements to increase the power of the 24 HP from 42 to the 49 bhp of the 1914 version, which was renamed the 20/30 HP in recognition of the changes. In the same way, the 15 HP gained an extra 6 hp, taking it to 28 bhp, and a new name: the Alfa 15/20 HP. But two things were happening which were threatening to halt the slow but genuine Alfa recovery. The pace of competition, even in the still relatively isolated Italian market, was hotting up; and

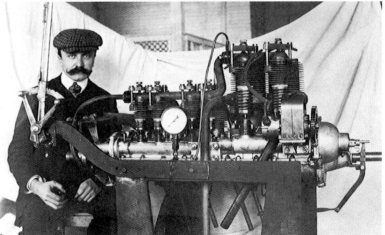

ABOVE *Merosi's career proved to be a remarkable one, spanning everything from bicycles to this power-driven compressor for the Italian army in the First World War. But despite several attempts, the one goal that proved too elusive was the production of a successful Grand Prix racing car.*

RIGHT *Soon after the 24 HP had gone into production, Merosi designed this slightly smaller and less powerful 15 HP variant which, despite its smaller engine and three-speed gearbox, was to prove equally popular. This 1911 version stands in the grounds of Alfa's Arese factory complex.*

the seemingly secure Europe of the early 20th century was edging closer and closer to the most catastrophic and appalling war it had ever experienced.

The first competition Alfa

Alfa had seen the first challenge coming a long time before. As early as 1911, the first full year of production, the directors had considered, and rejected, the idea of introducing an expensive new model to embody all the new ideas in design and performance. The spectre of increasing unreliability, and the possible loss of their small but loyal market, worried them so much that they decided instead to woo new customers by a more ambitious, although in those days less expensive and less risky step. Alfa would enter motor racing, and do this as simply as possible by producing a racing version of its original 24 HP model.

For a company to set out on a racing programme just a year after being rescued from collapse, and being set on the slow road to commercial recovery, was an astonishingly brave and confident thing to do. It was also astonishingly farsighted, since it established one aspect of the company's development that would hold good for the next three-quarters of a century. However, compared with some of the engineering challenges the company would meet and surmount later in its history, the actual mechanics of putting the decision into practice were still relatively simple.

Merosi began by cutting the car's heavy weight as much as he could. The alterations were modest enough: he shortened the ladder frame of the 24 HP, fitted the narrower axles used for the 12 HP model and stripped away all the bodywork apart from the bonnet, a pair of bucket seats for driver and passenger, two fuel tanks and a spare wheel. The result of all this was a modest drop in weight to 875 kg (1930 lb), and an equally modest increase in top speed to just under 114 km/h (70 mph). But the cut in weight improved the acceleration, the shorter wheelbase helped the handling, and the traditional reliability was still, he hoped, there in full measure.

Alfa began with the toughest challenge possible in the motor racing world of the time, where at least reliability mattered most. This was the Targa Florio, the epic race run through the mountains of northern Sicily for 444 km (276 miles) of the most gruelling conditions imaginable. The factory entered two of the new 24 HP Corsas, as the racing versions

LEFT The first true Alfa – Merosi's 24 HP was a revelation after the slow, unreliable and temperamental Darracqs which preceded it. Solid, reliable and spacious, it gave buyers (and the company's backers) new confidence in the marque. Performance would come later.

were called, and the joy was unbounded when one of them finished the first of the three 148 km (92-mile) marathon laps leading the race. But it was far too good to last: for once, the Sicilian skies produced a downpour, and the mud and the spray blinded both of the drivers, to the point where they had to retire.

This was disappointing, but only to be expected. Even before the First World War it was unusual for a new racing car to win first time out, especially against a challenge like this. When an Alfa was entered in the following year's Targa, changed for various reasons to a 1048 km (651-mile) marathon round the entire coast of the island, only to drop out with engine trouble (as did most of the field), it did nothing to shake the company's resolve. All it needed was something larger and more powerful to work with.

Success at last

Fortunately, Merosi had now been given permission to turn out a larger and more ambitious car to carry the Alfa badge. This was really an enlargement of the existing theme, but in view of the new importance of competition, he was able to bear sporting potential in mind from the start. The 40/60 HP, as the new car was called, had another four-cylinder engine, this time a 110 mm bore, 160 mm stroke, 6082 cc design with two basic differences from its predecessors. One was that, because of their size, the cylinders were cast in two pairs rather than as a single casting for all four. The other difference was much more important: instead of the side valves of the earlier engines, the 6-litre unit had overhead valves, mounted in the cylinder head itself. This meant the fuel–air mixture had a much shorter distance to travel into the cylinder when the inlet valve opened on each cycle, and the exhaust gases could be drawn out just as efficiently after the fuel was burned. The engine could therefore run fast, burn more fuel and develop more power: and with higher compression and twin carburettors, it was already developing a useful 73 bhp on test.

The 40/60 HP Corsa was built using the same methods as the smaller competition cars: by shortening and narrowing the frame and stripping away the bodywork of the production version, Alfa had a large but rugged racing machine capable of a promising 137 km/h (85 mph) and, if necessary, of keeping up that speed for hours on end. On its first outing, in the 53 km (33-mile) Parma to Poggio di Berceto hillclimb, a 40/60 won its class and put up second fastest time overall. Just behind it, and second in the class, was the other team car. Eight months later, in May 1914, two cars were entered in the Coppa Florio, run over the same Sicilian mountain course that had seen Alfa's first appearance in the Targa Florio three years before. They finished third and fourth overall, a brilliant and highly encouraging achievement.

The first Grand Prix Alfa

There is little doubt that the 40/60 HP had transformed Alfa's racing prospects, and a splendid career seemed to lie ahead for the car, and the team. But the management had its sights set on still higher targets – wins in hillclimbs and endurance races were all very well, but nothing captured the imagination of the general public as much as a victory in an international Grand Prix race. Then, as now, GP racing was the most glamorous, the most competitive, and the most dauntingly expensive type of racing for any company to enter. To contemplate developing a purpose-built car for this kind of challenge was either extremely brave, or amazingly rash, for such a young and financially shaky company.

As it was, there were some things the company clearly could not afford. Designing and building an entirely new chassis was out of the question – indeed, the main need was for a really powerful and competitive engine and, if Merosi's team could deliver that, the roadholding of the earlier competition cars was probably well up to the fairly primitive standards of the time. So the modifications were limited to shortening the frame by another 200 mm (8 in). The engine, however, was a different matter. Ruggedness and simplicity on their own were not enough. The whole design had to ensure efficiency to as high a degree as possible, and first and foremost this meant getting the fuel–air mixture into the cylinders, burning it, and removing the exhaust gases as quickly and smoothly as could be managed. Merosi therefore followed the best of engineering practice in putting the inlet and exhaust valves as close to the cylinders as possible – in the actual roof of the combustion chamber itself. But he arranged them in two rows, inclined at an angle and with each row driven by a separate camshaft (the engine-driven shafts which opened and closed each of the valves at the right moment in the cycle) mounted above it. Not only did this allow a pyramid-shaped combustion chamber, which was logical in terms of efficient burning of the fuel–air mixture, but it also allowed the valves themselves to be increased in size, which helped speed the gas flow in and out of the cylinders of the engine.

All of this made very sound sense – in fact, this prescription from

1914 was to govern the design of the world-beating racing Alfas of the 1950s and is still used in most of the production models today. But in the world of Grand Prix racing, an ounce of achievement outsells a ton of theory; the unit still had to prove it was powerful enough, and reliable enough, to live up to the promise of its design.

Alfa's race against time

The engine, however, was never to have this opportunity. First tests were encouraging, although far from conclusive: with 5.55 to 1 compression and two carburettors, it was delivering 88 bhp. This meant that Merosi's 100 mm bore, 143 mm stroke, 4492 cc racing engine was delivering 25 per cent more power than the 40/60 HP engine which was 35 per cent larger in capacity. But although that spoke volumes for the excellence of the new design, it was still true that cars were winning Grand Prix races at the time with substantially more power from engines of the same size. And if that was not enough, it had other handicaps. Alfa's ladder-frame chassis was within the weight limits allowed for Grand Prix racing, but was far too heavy to be competitive. At the same time the neatly cowled and streamlined body, although it looked fast and elegant, was too high, too broad and much too wasteful in the wind resistance it created to help the engine make up these deficiencies.

To be fair to Merosi, and Alfa, these problems were typical of those met by any team entering racing, and given time they would probably have been overcome. Yet time was the one ingredient Alfa lacked: the car was entered for the 1914 Circuit of Brescia meeting, and in the preliminary trials it clocked up 147.99 km/h (91.96 mph), which was far from disappointing. The race, however, was never run for, at the beginning of August, Germany invaded France and Belgium, and motor sport throughout Europe came to a sudden and complete stop. The car was put into storage to wait for more prosperous, and more settled, times.

For the time being, the only consolation for Italy was that she herself was clear of the fighting – and on the production front, Alfa's sales continued their slow but definite increase. From 20 cars turned out

LEFT *Merosi's Grand Prix Alfa of 1914 was too late for prewar events and too slow for postwar racing. Here Franchini is driving it to one of its few successes, a fourth place overall in the hotly contested Parma to Poggio di Berceto hillclimb of 1919: the overall winner was the measurably faster 1914 Grand Prix Fiat.*

works was helping to turn out tractors, aircraft engines and railway equipment as well as generators, and Romeo had bought out the other major shareholders to take over the company completely.

Just about the only thing the Alfa works did not make was cars. Romeo himself, although an enterprising engineer and successful businessman, was no car enthusiast, and parts for the last 105 cars had been stored away with no plans at all for turning them into complete vehicles. Yet history was to change that, as suddenly and dramatically as in 1914.

When the war came to an end in November 1918, Alfa technically did not exist at all. After Romeo's takeover the company had been renamed the Società Anonima Italiana Ing. Nicola Romeo, and Giuseppe Merosi had been given the job of running another of the

LEFT *Racing cars, in the days before 1914, were above all simple. All that was needed to turn Alfa's production 40/60 HP into a competition car was to pare away as much of the weight as possible. So the chassis frame of this 1913 car was shortened and narrowed and the bodywork cut to the minimum, with just bonnet, seats, petrol tank and spare wheels, to produce a potential winner. In time, the racing versions of the 40/60 and its stablemates were to make the company's reputation.*

during 1910, production had expanded to 80 the following year, to 150 in 1912, to more than 200 in 1913, to 272 in 1914 and to 205 in the first six months of 1915 alone. But the last figure is the most significant in only covering half a year. On 22 May 1915 Italy joined the Allies, and the fighting. Not surprisingly, production came to a halt and the company turned to other activities more relevant to the country's fight for survival against the onslaught of the Austro-Hungarian forces in the mountains to the north.

New crises and a new takeover

Merosi himself lost no time in adapting the 15/20 HP engine to work in a new role as a generator for the Italian army. But the old financial problems were now recurring from another direction. The last of the Darracq family to hold shares in the company, Alexandre's nephew Albert, had sold his holding to the Banca di Sconto. The bank was now worried that motor manufacturers – any motor manufacturers – were not the best of commercial bets in the middle of a world war, and so began to look for some way of spreading the risk.

Fortunately for the bank, and for Alfa, they found the very man in the industrialist and mining engineer Nicola Romeo, who was so busy making pumps and compressors for the army that he was actually looking for new investments and, even more important for his over-stretched business, new factory space. By the beginning of 1916 his turnover had expanded 24 times, and he was more than glad to buy some of the bank's Alfa shares and take over as managing director in return for the extra production capacity. Within two years, the Alfa

industrialist's plants in the south. But the return of peace meant the collapse of the market for army equipment, and while there was enough demand from the mining industry to keep the company afloat, it now had too much factory space that had stopped earning income. Nicola Romeo had become a prisoner of his own success. What use could he find for the workers and the plant now so suddenly made redundant?

Whatever his personal feelings, Romeo was far too seasoned an entrepreneur to overlook a real opportunity, and he knew full well the car market was bound to recover in time, although the need was for very different designs from the slow, solid, heavy and expensive prewar models. The first priority, however, was to turn out any cars at all; and the parts for the 105 production cars stored since the outbreak of war were to be priceless assets in winning a head start over the opposition.

Events moved quickly after that. Merosi came back from the south to pick up the production threads again. The cars were assembled and left the factory – 10 15/20 HPs, 95 20/30 HPs – to find ready buyers waiting for them, but they had one important difference from their prewar stablemates. Nicola Romeo had changed the name of the company, but in this specialized market he knew full well the value of reputation and continuity. Calling them Romeos would mean little outside the mining industry; calling them Alfas would hide the name of the new group of which the firm was now part. So a compromise was found, and a new name added to the company badge, with the cross-and-serpent crest of Milan as its centrepiece. Alfa, first renamed Romeo, had now become Alfa Romeo. The coming years were to make that new name far better known than the company's previous titles.

On the Move

Romeo had restarted production with the last of the prewar cars still in pieces in the factory. But although new designs would soon be needed, there was, he realized, one more urgent priority. The world outside had to be told, as loudly and clearly as possible, that the old firm was back in business and bound for success. There was only one way to do that, obvious even to a non-enthusiast, and that was to go back and start winning races, and so the competition programme began almost as soon as the first production cars were being assembled.

Three cars were entered for the first postwar Targa Florio, run at the end of 1919. Unfortunately, this was so late in the year that the Sicilian winter was well advanced, and once again the cars were drowned out in floods and a mudbath. Of 25 cars entered, 17 dropped out with mechanical problems of one kind or another, mostly brought on by the awesome conditions, and among them were the works Alfas of Franchini, Fracassi and Giuseppe Campari.

Other results were more encouraging. The 1919 Parma to Berceto hillclimb was won by the 1914 Grand Prix Fiat, but in fourth place overall and third in its class was the prewar Grand Prix Alfa, driven by Franchini. The following year, the touring car class in the event was won by a production 20/30 with Ugo Sivocci at the wheel and the racing car class by the competition version of the car, driven by Antonio Ascari. The massive 40/60 had now been better streamlined with new competition bodywork, and Campari drove it to victory in the over 6-litre class, winning equal second place overall. But a problem was that this model had been the first to be dropped from production, and so in future it would only be eligible for the more fiercely contested racing car classes, where it would have to fight very hard indeed for results.

In the 1920 Targa Florio the 40/60 failed to finish. But Alfa's growing reputation was saved by a smaller car, the 20/30 HP driven by a man whose name was soon to be as well known as that of the company, Enzo Ferrari. He had come to the team's notice by actually finishing the catastrophic 1919 race in a CMN car – he was, however, too late to qualify after being held up by police to allow the Provincial Governor to make a speech in the middle of the race – and he confirmed the

PREVIOUS PAGES *Large, handsome and imposing, a 1925 RL Super Sport poses against an appropriate background: the grounds of a villa near Arese*

ABOVE RIGHT *The 1923 RLTF (for Targa Florio) marked Alfa's first determined onslaught on the classic Sicilian endurance race, which the car won convincingly.*

RIGHT *This is the winning car on its way to victory, with Ugo Sivocci at the wheel, in the 1923 Targa Florio. Two other RLTFs finished second and fourth.*

accuracy of the firm's assessment of him by winning the touring car class and taking second place overall, just eight minutes behind the winner after eight and a half hours of racing.

As event succeeded event, production-based Alfas were doing better than their most committed followers would have predicted. But the Grand Prix car remained one of history's might-have-beens. After the war it had been fitted with a revised cylinder head with larger valves, which had helped boost its power peak to 102 bhp. In its final appearance, in the 1921 Brescia Speed Week, it led the 443 km (275-mile) Gran Premio Gentlemen ahead of Count Giulio Masetti's 115 bhp GP Mercedes, only to drop out with a catastrophic water leak on the last part of the last lap. The car had showed its promise too late. Only a completely new design would stand any real chance of winning racing's top honours: and in the meantime there were urgent priorities on the production front to be solved.

Merosi's first attempt at the postwar generation of production cars was a failure. Although the updated 20/30 HPs were selling well enough, the old 40/60 seemed to need a replacement at the larger end

of the market. He therefore took the existing chassis frame and lengthened it by 230 mm (9 in) and fitted bodywork of such imposing measurements that the dry weight of the car went up to a ton and a half, making it the heaviest Alfa yet, by a quite considerable margin. To power this leviathan he designed an entirely new six-cylinder engine, with the cylinders cast in two blocks of three, and 98 mm bores and a stroke of 140 mm, adding up to a capacity of 6330 cc. Yet for some reason, Merosi reverted to side valves and a single carburettor, so that the power output was a distinctly unambitious 70 bhp. This was enough to give the car a 112 km/h (70 mph) top speed, which was just enough – but the rest of the specification in terms of size, weight and luxury was entirely wrong for the time. The G1, as the car had been titled, had almost no sales at all in Italy, where the start of a capacity-based taxation torpedoed whatever appeal it might have had, and most of the 50 cars made went to reluctant export markets. Even a smaller capacity version, called the G2, was dropped as a certain nonstarter.

There was only one possibility as a replacement. Ever since the change in the Grand Prix racing rules, from the prewar capacity limit of

4.5 litres to a new one of 3 litres, had buried all hopes for an update of the 1914 car, the factory had been toying with a new design with which it could make a fresh start under the new rules. Oddly enough, it had taken several steps back from the old design: instead of inclined valves operated by twin overhead camshafts, it had overhead valves operated through pushrods and rockers, an efficient but far less appropriate arrangement for a GP car's power unit. This time the engine was another six-cylinder unit, with 75 mm cylinder bores and a 110 mm stroke, producing a 2916 cc capacity. With a single carburettor and 5.2 to 1 compression ratio the engine turned out 56 bhp, which was only a fraction less per cubic centimetre than the 1914 GP engine. However, there would have to be a great deal more development work on the engine before it had the slightest hope of becoming competitive, and before this could be done the racing formula was changed again, at the end of the 1921 season, to one of 2 litres.

Could this engine work in the opposite application, as a racing unit in a production car? Its pedigree promised much, but for some reason Alfa proceeded to load it down with a body larger and heavier than that of the ill-fated G1, and an extremely leisurely transmission with ratios spread so widely as to kill off whatever hopes of performance remained. The standard tourer reached a top speed of 110 km/h (68 mph), slower than the more sporting prewar cars.

All the same, from a beginning like this the new RL could only get better. It was at least reliable, and its smaller capacity meant that the customers could have mediocre performance at a lower cost in fuel and taxes, so it began to sell. But the RL's real significance was in the family that it fathered. Although the Grand Prix hopes of the design had been blighted, there were still prospects in the sports car arena, and Merosi was developing an RL Sport version, with wider 76 mm cylinder bores, a capacity of 2994 cc, larger valves, stronger connecting rods, higher compression ratio and power increased to 72 bhp, an improvement of more than 20 per cent. When this was matched by a chassis shortened by 305 mm (12 in) and lightened by 50 kg (110 lb), the top speed climbed to 130 km/h (80 mph) and the performance of the car was transformed.

Alfa's sales prospects were to be transformed in the same way. The new cars, the RLN (for RL Normale) and the RLS (for RL Sport), had appeared in the closing weeks of 1921, and at the end of the year three examples of each car had been built. But by the end of 1922 more than 800 RLs had been turned out, which meant that the company's Portello works had produced almost as many cars in twelve months as they had in the five years leading up to the wartime shut-down.

There was more to come: the pointed radiator which distinguished the Sport version from the standard RL was inherited by its successor, the RL Super Sport (or RLSS) of 1925. This had a still more powerful 86 bhp version of the 3-litre six, and with a closer-ratio gearbox even the production model was good for more than 130 km/h (80 mph).

By this time, however, two things had happened. The sporting programme had boomed, with competition versions of the RL taking over from their essentially prewar-based predecessors. The first RL to be entered in Alfa's traditional proving ground for its competition cars, the Targa Florio, failed even to finish. But fortunately the Alfa team went on to use the design as a basis for a more specialized version altogether. They shortened the chassis frame by 305 mm (12 in) and covered it with a tiny and carefully streamlined racing body, with frontal area cut to the minimum and panelling shaped around the two bucket seats, the fuel tanks and the spare wheels. The engine was given a higher compression ratio and lightened valve gear to boost the power to 88 bhp, and three works cars were produced to this specification; two more were built with special engines of 78 mm cylinder bore and a capacity of 3154 cc, which increased the power still further to 95 bhp. Lightened bodies, better streamlining and close-ratio gearboxes helped produce top speeds of 145 (90) and 158 km/h (98 mph) for the two versions of the RLTF (RL Targa Florio), which was the official designation for the works cars.

The result was that one of the machines, driven by Ugo Sivocci, won the race, with Ascari second and Count Masetti fourth. The cars went on to win a series of other sports car races, and the following year they were succeeded by a more powerful version still. The 1924 RLTFs had bores widened to 80 mm and a long-throw crankshaft which increased

RIGHT *Alfa triumphed again at the Targa Florio in 1930, after years of Bugatti domination, but it took a specially modified P2 Grand Prix racing car, and a driver of the skill of Achille Varzi, to do it.*

BELOW *For 1924, the RLTFs were uprated and fitted with differently shaped body panelling. Again the cars did well, although overall victory eluded them. This particular car, pictured at Silverstone, was brought to England in 1925 and still races regularly. Provided by Chris Mann.*

Alfa Romeo P2

Years made	1924–30
No. made	6

ENGINE

Type	In-line, water-cooled
No. of cylinders	8
Bore/stroke mm	61 × 85
Displacement cc	1987
Valve operation	2 rows of inclined valves in roof of combustion chamber, actuated directly by twin overhead camshafts
Sparkplugs per cyl.	1
Compression ratio	6:1
Induction	2 downdraught carburettors and engine-driven supercharger
BHP	140–175 at 5500 rpm

DRIVE TRAIN

Clutch	Multiple dry-plate
Transmission	4-speed gearbox with propeller shaft to rear axle

CHASSIS

Frame	C-section girders in modified ladder frame
Weight	750 kg (1654 lb)
Wheelbase	2630 mm (8 ft 7½ in)
Track – front	1300 mm (4 ft 3 in)
Track – rear	1200 mm (3 ft 11¼ in)
Suspension	Semi-elliptic leaf springs
Brakes	Drums, rod-operated
Tyre size – front	19 × 5.25
Tyre size – rear	19 × 6.00
Wheels	Spoked, centre-lock

PERFORMANCE

Maximum speed	225 km/h (140 mph)

The 1924 P2 was the car that crowned Alfa's efforts for Grand Prix success by winning its first World Championship.

the stroke to 120 mm, the capacity to 3620 cc, and the power to 125 bhp. The RLTFs had long louvred bonnets (hoods) with the pointed radiators of the production models, and slab tails carrying the spare wheels and the fuel tanks. They had drum brakes on all four wheels, and a top speed of 177 km/h (110 mph). Although they narrowly failed to win the 1924 Targa after a razor's edge finish, they secured second, fourth and ninth places, followed once again by a succession of other victories.

Grand Prix hopes again

By this time, however, the Grand Prix programme had been revived all over again, and Merosi was able to start from the much-needed clean sheet of paper to produce a result that would be truly competitive. The car was originally designated the GPR (for Grand Prix Romeo) but has been known ever since as the Alfa Romeo P1. It had the usual girder frame, but reduced by fully 450 mm (18 in) from that of the RL, and carefully curved to follow the contours of the streamlined racing body, the panelling of which was shaped from aluminium to save weight still further. The car turned the scales at 850 kg (1875 lb), which was better than Alfa's earlier efforts but still heavy by Grand Prix standards. As against that, the engine was more ambitious than the earlier designs: this time Merosi had chosen the classic inclined valves and twin overhead camshaft layout of the 1914 unit, with some important innovations. To save weight the six-cylinder unit was assembled from separate cylinder liners with the two halves of the block welded up from sheet steel, bolted to a crankcase cast in light alloy. With 7.3 to 1

compression ratio and twin carburettors, the 1990 cc (65 × 100 mm) engine turned out some 80 bhp. This figure was at least encouraging for the future.

In the event, however, the car's future was all too soon its past. Although it was capable of more than 177 km/h (110 mph), and the company felt confident enough to enter all three of the cars it had built for the 1923 Italian Grand Prix, tragedy was waiting at the trackside. Ugo Sivocci was testing the first of the cars on the Monza circuit when he slid off the track on the Curva Vialone and was killed in the ensuing crash. Alfa withdrew the other two cars as a mark of respect, the GP was won by Fiat, and the two surviving P1s never ran again.

New designs from a new designer

By 1925, and the appearance of the RLSS as the last link in the RL chain, it was clear that the buyers, too, needed something new to keep them happy. Although the cars had done well, backed up by an equivalent range of four-cylinder models, designated RM, which sold in much smaller numbers, the figures were now beginning to fall off quite alarmingly. Again, and happily for Alfa's fortunes, the answer was very close to being ready – and the amazing truth is that the new production car, which was to become one of the most famous and most desirable of all the Alfas, was to owe its origins to the design that would bring the company the much-sought-after and most elusive Grand Prix success after so much waiting and so much effort.

The man responsible for these two versions of the same basic design was a new addition to the Alfa Romeo ranks. Indeed, at the time when

20

Merosi's P1 was taking shape, he was working for the Fiat team that led the Grand Prix world as far as Italy was concerned, and won the race for which the P1s had been entered. His name was Vittorio Jano, and he turned out to be a friend and colleague of a man called Luigi Bazzi. The latter had left Fiat after an argument with the chief racing engineer to go and work on the Alfa racing team with his old friend Enzo Ferrari.

Although Bazzi was a valuable acquisition, he did not have the appropriate depth of experience, particularly with the newest techniques of superchargers (engine-driven compressors that forced the fuel–air mixture into the cylinders under pressure to increase speed and power) which were then becoming essential in racing. But he knew the man who did: none other than Vittorio Jano. So Bazzi suggested that efforts should be made to persuade Jano to leave Turin, where the Fiat racing team was based, and to come and work for Alfa in Milan.

The negotiations were long and delicate, involving Ferrari himself as a go-between, but finally resulted in Jano taking over in the Alfa workshops, where from the beginning his priceless experience galvanized the process of racing development with a new sense of urgency. His new car when it took shape was in its basics quite close to the ideas that Merosi had been developing, but the added ingredient of hard-won knowledge gained on the racing circuits soon made itself apparent.

The power unit, for example, owed a great deal to the Fiat 805 racing engine on which Jano had been working at Turin. It was a straight-8 with hemispherical combustion chambers, two rows of inclined valves set in the roof of the combustion chambers and operated by two overhead camshafts, and every precaution was taken to make the engine as strong as possible without harming performance and output. The long crankshaft was made in two pieces and carefully counterbalanced to reduce rotating loads, and was carried in no fewer than ten roller bearings. Even the overhead camshafts were carried in ten bearings apiece, and roller bearings were also used for the big ends. The bores were set at 61 mm which, with a stroke of 85 mm, produced a capacity of 1987 cc, comfortably under the 2-litre limit.

Jano knew from the beginning the engine would be supercharged, and to keep this vital part of the design directly under his control he had

forged openings in the axle, as they did on the Fiat GP car, and the rear leaf springs, too, were almost completely enclosed in the compact bodywork. The body panelling itself was smaller than the P1's in frontal area and the weight was 120 kg (265 lb) less, even with the extra penalty of having to carry the supercharger, putting the car just above the minimum limit.

This was Alfa's most formidable GP challenge yet, and with a single carburettor the first car was turning out 134 bhp on test, with more to come. On 9 June 1924, Ascari took the new car out on the Circuit of Cremona, where it won convincingly. By early August a team of four was entered for the Grand Prix of Europe, to be run at Lyon in France against the fierce opposition of four professional and highly competitive teams: Fiat, Delage, Bugatti and Sunbeam. Yet the result was better than anyone could have hoped: Ferrari's car had to be scratched because its driver was ill; Ascari's led the race until a water leak put it out of the running with the distance three-quarters run; and Wagner's car finished fourth. But Campari won the race against the toughest opposition in Europe, and won it so convincingly that Fiat withdrew on the spot, having heard the bells toll the end of its 20-year record of victories at events all over the Continent.

This was recompense at last for the years of wasted efforts and blighted hopes: but for Alfa there was much more to come. Jano developed a faster and more powerful twin-carburettor version in time for the Italian GP at Monza in October, where the chief opponents would be Mercedes – but a fatal accident caused the Mercedes team to withdraw, and the Alfa team finished first, second, third and fourth. So impressive had the cars' speed and clockwork-like reliability proved that Jano decided to subordinate everything else to contesting the 1925 championship. The works sports cars were sold off to private owners and the team concentrated on preparing for just three events: the European Grand Prix at Spa in Belgium, the French GP and the Italian GP. Once again the cars were improved by boosting the power, and by increasing the fuel tank capacity to reduce the need for pit stops.

At Spa one of the P2s, driven by Count Gastone Brilli-Peri, dropped out with a broken front spring, but all the Delages followed suit with

LEFT *Jano's Championship-winning straight-8 Grand Prix engine, when shorn of two cylinders, provided the power unit for a splendid series of sporting six-cylinder cars, which were to become the most famous and most desirable Alfas of all. This is a 6C 1500 of 1928; later versions ranged up to 1900 cc.*

RIGHT *The six-cylinder cars were to prove as successful on the racing track as they were in the showroom. This one, another 6C 1500, is being driven by Enzo Ferrari. He started as a driver for Alfa and went on to manage the racing team, and was largely responsible for many of its prewar successes.*

the lobe-type blower made in Alfa's own workshops. Geared to run at 1.25 times engine speed, it was tried out in one of the P1s, where it boosted the power to 118 bhp, an increase of more than 20 per cent, and pushed the top speed to 200 km/h (125 mph). But in the new car, now called the P2, it should do even better, since the other aspect of the design was to produce a chassis as light and efficient as possible.

Here again there were surface similarities to the P1 in that the frame was built up of a ladder of C-section girders, and the wheels were carried on semi-elliptic leaf springs front and rear. However, there were many important differences. The front springs passed through

blower problems. The other two P2s of Ascari and Campari finished first and second, the only two cars to complete the fast and gruelling race. Then tragedy struck in the French GP: Ascari carried on in driving rain on worn tyres, skidded off the road and suffered a fatal crash. The team withdrew immediately, leaving Delage to take first and second places. The Italian GP saw Campari's Alfa take the lead after the third lap and hold it for 320 km (200 miles) until he had to stop at the pits – but it was Brilli-Peri in another P2 who took over to win. with Campari in second place and the third P2 coming in fifth. So in its first full season of Grand Prix racing Alfa had taken the World

Championship, a magnificent achievement by any standards. As a mark of celebration, the company's badge on all its cars was circled by a laurel wreath, a feature it wore until recently.

This was a wonderful moment, after the years of disappointment, frustration and missed opportunities. But already there were other priorities claiming the attention of both Jano and the company. The sporting programme, whatever the excitement and the rewards it provided, was essentially only an aid to selling cars, and in that respect the company's performance had been starting to flag – ironically, at the very time of its greatest track success. What was needed now was a car good enough to capitalize on that success and win the customers back, and one that would be ready as quickly as Jano's ingenuity and the hard work of his team could produce it.

Over the years since the 1920s, the argument that racing car improvements have a direct and immediate effect on production cars has been discredited, as the racers themselves have become more sophisticated. But even in the 1920s there was so much difference between a sucessful Grand Prix car and the average showroom model, even from a sporting manufacturer, that Jano's radical solution to the urgent problems facing the company was exceedingly bold.

What he did was simple enough to describe; but much less so to carry through in reality. He took the world-beating P2 and made a production sports car out of it. By taking off the supercharger, and by removing two of the cylinders from the engine, he produced an unblown six-cylinder engine of 1.5 litres capacity, but still blessed with the efficiency allowed by an overhead camshaft, and overhead valves opening into a combustion chamber composed of a flat top and a domed recess in the crown of the piston.

The power unit would need this kind of efficiency, for here was a car intended to provide performance with a much smaller engine than was normal. Sports car builders, free of the artificial restrictions imposed by racing formulae, usually opted for larger engines and lower stresses to provide the power. And here was Jano employing an engine that was actually smaller than the 2-litre unit used in the admittedly unsparkling RM, smaller sister of the RL series.

All the same, the P2's performance had shown how much could be achieved by careful weight reduction. In the case of the new car, designated originally the NR (for Nicola Romeo), although the ladder-frame chassis was much the same size as the RM's, its weight, at 1000 kg (2200 lb), was only two-thirds that of the earlier car. The engine in its original form delivered a useful but not very exciting 44 bhp, and was fitted into two basic models: the standard wheelbase version and a larger long-wheelbase tourer. Both used four-speed gearboxes, rod-operated drum brakes on all four wheels, friction

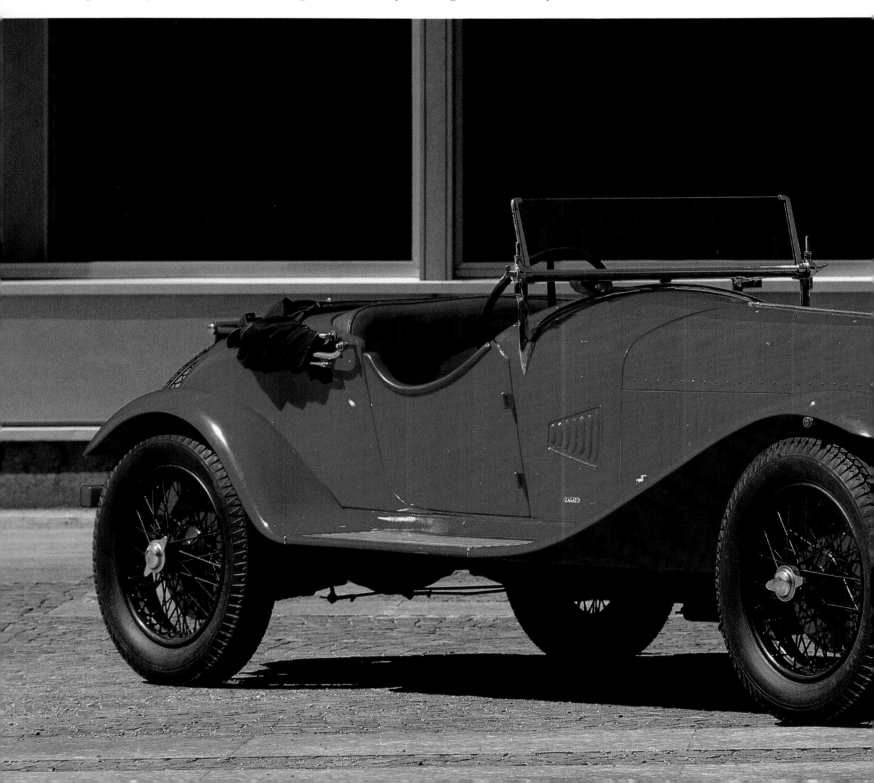

BELOW *The brilliant Tazio Nuvolari had some of his greatest races in Alfas, like this 6C 1750 in the 1930 Targa – which Varzi won in the P2.*

BOTTOM *The beautiful 6C 1750 Gran Sport was probably the most popular and successful of all the Jano six-cylinder cars. Half a century later, more than any other design, it still epitomizes the grace, balance, elegance and quality of the sporting Alfa Romeos of the 1930s.*

dampers and semi-elliptic leaf springs for front and rear suspension.

The prototypes of the 6C 1500, as the car had been renamed, appeared during the spring of 1925, when the P2 was on its way to its World Championship. But production was delayed until 1927, when 200 of the cars were made: the fact that three-quarters of them were the heavier and slower long-wheelbase version showed that whatever was selling the car, it was not performance. The brilliant asset of Alfa's racing success was being wasted without a genuinely sporting version of the car to turn it into increasing sales figures.

Happily for the company this was not long in coming. The 6C 1500 was the founder of a dynasty of brilliant sporting models which have become classics in automotive history for their speed, reliability, sporting prowess, and above all for their sheer style and beauty. These cars have probably become more identified with the name of Alfa than any other of its products in the years since 1910, and they command astronomical prices among collectors today.

The progression started slowly enough – in 1928 the 1500 Sport appeared, with the same engine except for a return to the twin overhead camshafts and the hemispherical conbustion chambers of the P2. This pushed the power up to 54 bhp, and the top speed to 125 km/h (78 mph). But the real excitement began with the 6C 1500 SS (Super Sport), which had a shorter wheelbase to reduce weight and improve

Alfa Romeo 6C 1750 Gran Sport

Years made	1929–33
No. made	257

ENGINE

Type	In-line
No. of cylinders	6
Bore/stroke mm	65 × 88
Displacement cc	1752
Valve operation	2 rows of inclined valves in roof of combustion chambers, directly actuated by twin overhead camshafts
Sparkplugs per cyl.	1
Compression ratio	5:1
Induction	1 horizontal carburettor with twin-lobe Alfa Romeo supercharger running at engine speed
BHP	85 at 4500 rpm

DRIVE TRAIN

Clutch	Multiple dry-plate
Transmission	4-speed manual gearbox, propeller shaft to rear axle

CHASSIS

Frame	C-section girders in ladder frame
Weight	920 kg (2028 lb)
Wheelbase	2745 mm (9 ft 1 in)
Track	1380 mm (4 ft 6 in)
Suspension	Semi-elliptic leaf springs
Brakes	Drums on all 4 wheels, rod-operated
Tyre size	28 × 5.25
Wheels	Spoked, centre-lock

PERFORMANCE

Maximum speed	145 km/h (90 mph)

handling, a neat two-seater body, a higher compression 60 bhp engine and a top speed of 130 km/h (80 mph). Keen buyers could specify a valuable optional extra: a supercharger which, although less powerful than the unit fitted to the P2, still managed to boost power to 76 bhp and top speed to 140 km/h (87 mph).

Preoccupied with developing the new cars, Alfa Romeo had withdrawn from racing after winning the Championship. However, the sporting potential of the new models had already begun to win favour with private owners, who were entering them in all kinds of sprints, races and hillclimbs. Bit by bit, Alfa came to realize the value of helping these enthusiastic amateurs and, in time, of re-entering the sporting world itself, in cars that once again bore the clearest resemblance to the ordinary production versions.

It all began with the very first Mille Miglia, the epic 1600 km (1000-mile) road race through Italy, run in 1927. Alfa entered two RL Super Sports in the event. Both retired, although Gastone Brilli-Peri had actually led the race at one time. The following year, however, Giuseppe Campari and Giulio Ramponi, in the only works 6C 1500 entered, triumphed against much more formidable opposition and actually won the race outright.

The car they used was a special version with a fixed cylinder head and larger valves, which developed 84 bhp – almost twice the output of the original version of the engine. But the new works effort, and the enthusiastic private owners, were soon to have even more powerful weaponry at their disposal, when the 1500 series gave way to the immortal 1750s.

Here, too, the prescription was simple enough to describe: Jano widened the cylinder bores to 65 mm and lengthened the stroke to 86 mm to increase the capacity to 1752 cc. The oddest feature of the new car, however, was that Alfa followed rigidly the progression of the earlier model: the original 1750 reverted to the single-cam version of the engine, with a 46 bhp power output which was only very slightly better than its predecessor and was, in any case, cancelled out by a corresponding increase in weight.

Birth of the GT and return of the P2

Fortunately for the enthusiasts, and for Alfa's growing sporting reputation, the new versions were not long in coming; and in this case the larger engine of the 1750 gave ample scope for development. The Sport version was succeeded by the Super Sport and by a new variant called the Gran Sport which became the top of the range. In its production form, aided by a supercharger, the open sports version turned out 85 bhp and could top 145 km/h (90 mph). This ample power output meant that a new breed of car, and a new term to describe it, was just

ABOVE *Not all the 1750s were open two-seaters: the chassis were sold to a variety of different bodybuilders and many were fitted with closed or drophead body styles, like this 1750 GT coupé by James Young, combining performance with comfort. Provided by Geoffrey Wilson.*

LEFT *Amazingly, even the more opulent Turismo and Gran Turismo variants entered races, like this 1929 6C 1750 Turismo at Brescia.*

around the corner: a close-coupled saloon with a slightly heavier body but a still sparkling 135 km/h (84 mph) became the 1750 Gran Turismo. Then, finally, the works racing versions were delivering 102 bhp and reaching a top speed of 171 km/h (106 mph), with handling and acceleration to match.

What all this meant in sales terms was a steady climb in the production figures. What it signified in sporting terms was a succession of wins in every kind of event: Campari and Ramponi won the 1929 Mille Miglia in a 1750 and Tazio Nuvolari, one of the greatest racing drivers of all time, beat his arch-rival Achille Varzi to do the same a year later. The only way he could sneak up on his alert team mate and carry off the victory was to race down a mountain pass in the dark on sidelights alone, trusting to his sharp reflexes to avoid disaster.

The only event the 1750s failed to win was the Targa Florio, which in the late 1920s had become a Bugatti benefit. At the end of the decade, however, Alfa was to add this classic race to its list of honours, and this was to provide Varzi with his revenge for being beaten in the Mille Miglia. But it was to take a very special car to do it: a rebuilt version of

the P2 with wider cylinder bores, revised suspension, 1750 wheels and axles, and lower and leaner bodies based much more closely on the sports cars. Running this thinly disguised Grand Prix racing car on the Sicilian mountain circuit seemed a certain route to disaster, and Jano himself advised against it. However, Varzi was determined, reasoning that only the racing car's fearsome 175 bhp output could compensate for the Bugattis' superb handling.

In the end it was a brilliant victory, but not without its heart-stopping moments. The highly tuned engine burned fuel at a disconcerting rate, and a leak in the fuel tank meant that the car would run out unless the mechanic topped it up from can and funnel at speed. Inevitably a few drops spilled on the hot exhaust and the tail of the car caught fire, but Varzi kept on going, trailing flames and smoke behind him, to win the race in record time. It put an end for ever to Bugatti domination of the Targa: the French company never won the event again. From now on Alfa was to make the event its own with an even more crushing succession of victories.

Great things lay ahead on the production front, too, with a series of brilliant designs from Jano's fertile imagination. The company's greatest successes may have lain in the future, but so, too, did its greatest challenges. In the year that saw the culmination of the production car development and the triumphant return of the P2 to crown a sporting record second to none, events on the other side of the world had already set in motion an economic crisis which was to bring the company to the brink of disaster for the third time in its short but remarkable existence.

Sports Cars for the State

As the 1920s gave way to the 1930s, Alfa's success seemed assured. Jano and his team were already working on the eventual successor to the already outstandingly successful 1500s and 1750s, a design that would be bigger, more powerful and more expensive than either. All the market trends pointed to this type of car being in the greatest demand as the decade advanced, and it was time for Alfa to ensure a share of this lucrative business. But, as before, the problem lay in evolving a new design as simply, and as efficiently, as Jano's ingenuity could make possible.

His answer, as always, showed the clarity and the brilliance of engineering genius. Just as the removal of two cylinders had paved the way for converting the P2 Grand Prix engine into the power unit for the six-cylinder sports cars, so the same process in reverse would produce another straight-8. The inspiration, however, lay in the detail differences. Jano took the 1750 version of the six-cylinder engine, and instead of simply adding two cylinders on the end of the engine, he cut the engine in half, producing two four-cylinder units, which he then turned round and joined together again back-to-back. This meant that the long camshafts and crankshafts required for an eight-cylinder in-line engine were no longer necessary. The new engine had the camshaft drives and all the auxiliaries in the centre; instead of, for example, one long crankshaft working with all eight cylinders, there were now two shorter crankshafts with four cylinders apiece. These were joined in the centre through a set of helical gears, which also drove the dynamo, the oil and water pumps, the supercharger and the four overhead camshafts, two for each bank of four cylinders.

This, for once, was to be a sporting car from the beginning, so that reliability at high performance levels was absolutely essential. Having gone to such pains to avoid the whip and vibration that might occur in long crankshafts and camshafts, Jano then took equally great care that the engine's shorter shafts would be so well supported that no problems would arise in this quarter: each camshaft was carried in six bronze bearings, and each crankshaft in five main bearings, which was equivalent to ten main bearings for the whole engine. But the trouble taken was rewarded by a power output of 138 bhp, or more power for an equivalent size of engine than the works racing 1750s, and the development story had hardly started!

The progress on the engine was matched by the design of the rest of the car. Nicola Romeo had retired from running the company in 1928, and one result may have been the disappearance of any need for a mundane bottom-of-the-range version with underpowered engine and overwhelming bodywork. This time the bodies were as sleek and refined as the mechanicals: a short-wheelbase version little larger than the 1750 called the Corto; and a larger and more imposing, although still not over-heavy variant, called the Lungo.

The 2300 in competition

From the beginning, the 2300s were set for competition honours. The first works cars appeared in 1931, with uprated superchargers, larger valves and a power output of 155 bhp, and although they failed to finish the Mille Miglia of that year, this was due to problems with tyres rather than with the cars. To prove the point, the team won the Targa Florio and then went on to take the 1932 Mille Miglia as well. There was even better to come: in 1931, the Grand Prix rules were changed to allow cars of any design at all, provided that they had two seats, carried no mechanics and lasted out for races of at least ten hours' duration.

It seemed as if the 2300, with its flexibility and reliability, could have been designed with these new regulations in mind. The team began the modifications that would turn the development wheel full circle, so that Jano's design had gone from a straight-8 Grand Prix car to a six-cylinder sports car, to an eight-cylinder sports car and back to an eight-cylinder Grand Prix car again. This final step in the progression was a highly tuned 2300 with higher compression, larger valves, more boost from the supercharger and streamlined racing bodywork. A fortnight after the Mille Miglia win the first two of these Grand Prix 2300s were entered in the Grand Prix of Europe, to be run at Monza. They finished first and second, and this version of the car was always afterwards to be known as the Monza in honour of that first-time victory.

PREVIOUS PAGES *Following the success of the six-cylinder sports cars, Jano returned to the eight-cylinder theme with a completely new engine design (effectively two four-cylinder units set back-to-back) for the powerful and imposing 8C 2300. This splendid example of the close-coupled two-seater version was provided by J.C. Bamford Excavators Ltd.*

RIGHT *The 2300 sports car provided the engine and chassis for a racing version which was named the Monza, in honour of its first victory in the 1932 Grand Prix of Europe. When Alfa had to withdraw the P3s from racing, the works team fell back on the Monza, which proved a brilliant stopgap. This ex-team car is still raced regularly. Provided by Paul Grist.*

The freedom of the racing rules, however, was to have one inevitable result: a power race began, with the teams turning to larger and larger engines in attempts to steal a march on the opposition. In time this would limit itself because of the greater weights of the larger units, and the difficulty of ensuring that the extra power could be coped with by the crude suspensions of the time. But for the time being, the Monza's 2.3 litres would not be enough and for Grand Prix racing, at least, something else was needed.

The initial stopgap was based on the idea utilized in the Sedici Cilindri Maserati, evolved to meet the same need to provide ample power without the time, trouble and expense of designing and developing a new, bigger unit: the idea was to use two engines instead. In Alfa's case, Jano designed a new racing car called the Tipo A which had two 1750 engines mounted side by side, and modified to turn in opposite directions so as to cancel out the torque reactions. Each engine was connected to its own gearbox and clutch, and a complicated series of linkages allowed the driver to control it all through a single gear lever and a single clutch pedal.

The car produced a total of 115 bhp from each engine, which put it well up in the power stakes. It was, however, extremely difficult to handle – so difficult that on its first test outing a driver called Luigi Arcangeli skidded off the track at Monza and was killed. All the same, Campari was able to win the Coppa Acerbo in one of these cars, and in

doing so he beat the big 4.9-litre Bugattis which had been uncatchable before then.

It was clearly time for a compromise: the Monza in its original version had handled well and proved supremely reliable but had lacked enough power to be competitive against bigger-engined opposition. The Tipo A had power in plenty but had handling problems, and also proved prone to breakdowns. What was needed was a car with the toughness and roadholding of the Monza with some of the extra power of the Tipo A. To produce it, Jano once again went back to the P2, or more exactly its latest descendant.

He took the Monza engine and lengthened the stroke to 100 mm, and increased the capacity to 2654 cc. He fitted larger valves, inclined at a wider angle to fit into a revised cylinder head, and he fitted a pair of blowers instead of the single supercharger used previously. The power output climbed to 215 bhp, or very little less than the 230 bhp of the unwieldy Tipo A, and to make the best possible use of this extra power, Jano capitalized on another change in the racing rules. From 1932 onwards, the seat for the non-essential mechanic was no longer compulsory, and the car could be a true single-seater at last.

This allowed the rear end of the car to be redesigned. The body could be lighter, sleeker, narrower and more compact, but the problem was still in the irreducible height needed to mount the driver's seat above the propeller shaft linking the gearbox to the rear axle. Jano managed to effect a useful improvement by shifting the differential forward next to the gearbox, and then driving the rear wheels through a pair of propeller shafts, each one angled outwards to one of the rear wheels, to which it was connected through bevel gears. This unorthodox divided drive had three advantages: the transmission was easier to reach for maintenance or for changing the gear ratios to suit different conditions; by repositioning the differential and mounting it on the chassis, the unsprung weight of the rear axle was reduced to the weight of the wheels and their associated bevel gears – this improved the roadholding; and finally it allowed the driver's seat to be lowered slightly to bring about a useful reduction in overall height and frontal area.

Alfa Romeo 8C 2600 Monza	
Years made	1933–4
No. made	6 (some earlier 2300s were converted to 2600s)
ENGINE	
Type	In-line
No. of cylinders	8
Bore/stroke mm	68 × 88
Displacement cc	2556
Valve operation	2 rows of inclined valves in roof of combustion chamber, actuated directly by twin overhead camshafts
Sparkplugs per cyl.	1
Compression ratio	6.5:1
Induction	1 downdraught carburettor and twin-lobe Alfa Romeo supercharger driven at 1.428 times engine speed
BHP	180 at 5600 rpm
DRIVE TRAIN	
Clutch	Multiple dry-plate
Transmission	4-speed gearbox with propeller shaft to rear axle
CHASSIS	
Frame	C-section girders in modified ladder frame
Weight	920 kg (2028 lb)
Wheelbase	2650 mm (8 ft 8 in)
Track	1380 mm (4 ft 6 in)
Suspension	Semi-elliptic leaf springs
Brakes	Drums on all 4 wheels, rod-operated
Tyre size	29 × 5.50
Wheels	Spoked, centre-lock
PERFORMANCE	
Maximum speed	225 km/h (140 mph)

Alfa Romeo Tipo B Monoposto (P3)

Years made	1932–3
No. made	6

ENGINE

Type	In-line
No. of cylinders	8
Bore/stroke mm	65 × 100
Displacement cc	2654
Valve operation	2 rows of inclined valves in roof of combustion chambers actuated by twin overhead camshafts
Sparkplugs per cyl.	1
Compression radio	6.5:1
Induction	2 downdraught carburettors, and 2 twin-lobe super-chargers, running at 1.448 times engine speed
BHP	215 at 5600 rpm

DRIVE TRAIN

Clutch	Multiple dry-plate
Transmission	4-speed manual with divided drive to rear wheels

CHASSIS

Frame	Longitudinal and transverse box sections, welded from sheet steel
Weight	700 kg (1540 lb)
Wheelbase	2650 mm (8 ft 8 in)
Track – front	1380 mm (4 ft 6 in)
Track – rear	1300 mm (4 ft 3 in)
Suspension	Semi-elliptic leaf springs
Brakes	Drums on all 4 wheels, rod-operated
Tyre size	19 × 6.00
Wheels	Wire, centre-lock

PERFORMANCE

Maximum speed	232 km/h (144 mph)

The beautiful P3: one of the most elegant GP cars ever. This example was updated by the works team in 1934 with quarter-elliptic rear suspension. Provided by Chris Mann and Henry Wessells III.

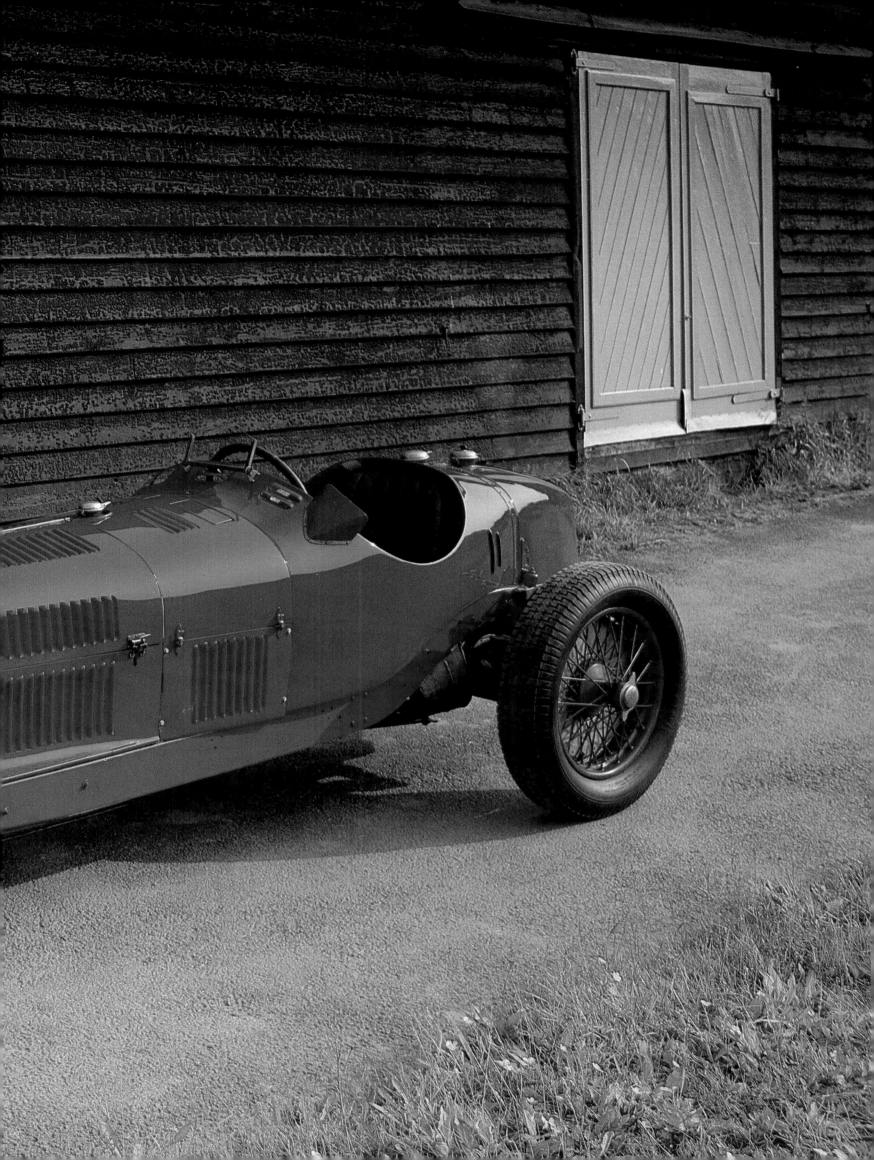

RIGHT *Alfa's response to the collapse of its traditional markets in the 1930s was a cheaper and simpler car – the 6C 2300 – which would appeal to a wider circle of less well-off customers. This is the 1934 Gran Turismo version. In the background is the former home of Count Ricotti, himself an Alfa enthusiast of long standing, who commissioned one of the first aerodynamic bodies – on the ALFA 40/60.*

BELOW *Vittorio Jano, who had been responsible for Fiat's all-conquering racing department, was to do the same for Alfa Romeo until the might of the government-backed German teams was to prove irresistible. But his brilliant succession of production cars did even more to make the company's reputation during the 1930s.*

No other detail was forgotten in the fight to save weight, including the use of light alloys for both cylinder blocks and chassis frame. The result was the Alfa Romeo P3, a car that not only looked supremely fast and graceful, but had a really promising specification. Its chief rivals, the big Bugattis, had engines of twice the capacity, but the meagre 40 bhp power advantage they enjoyed was swallowed up by the extra 180 kg (397 lb) body weight they carried and their less efficient roadholding.

32

Back to Grands Prix

The 1932 season saw the Alfa team's return to Grand Prix racing after an absence of seven years: the cars failed to score overall wins at Marseille in France and at Brno, Czechoslovakia, but in every other event they entered they won, against the toughest and most formidable opposition in the world. It seemed that nothing could stop Alfa Romeo on its way to total domination of every branch of international motor sport: nothing, that is, except a major financial crash – which was exactly what happened. So short of money was the company that the racing programme was abruptly cancelled, and the works P3s were put into storage, their splendid story over before it had really begun.

Coming challenges had already cast their shadows at the time when Jano was busy developing the 2300. The first ripples caused by the Wall Street crash across the Atlantic had started to worry investors in Italy, among them the Banca di Sconto, still a large shareholder in the company and still, it seemed, concerned about its viability – despite the fact that the other Romeo companies were thriving on government contracts for army vehicles and aero engines under Mussolini's armament drive. In the end it was the Italian government itself, as the Romeo group's biggest customer, that stepped in and took over the bank's shareholding. The company's cash crisis was solved, for the time being at least, and Jano was able to go ahead and produce his masterpieces without further interruptions.

The trouble was that the world itself was changing, and the market for which the 2300s had been developed was vanishing like water

keep the company afloat. New cars would be made, better suited to the new market's requirements but, in the meantime, the first priority was to revive the racing programme so as to realize the maximum return on the capital spent.

Six months is not a long time to mount such a complex financial operation: but in Grand Prix racing it can be long enough to change conditions out of all recognition. While the P3s had been retired from the tracks, Scuderia Ferrari had been reduced to competing with Monzas and racing versions of the 2300s, and had done well with this less than competitive material. However, in the time between the end of the triumphant 1932 season and the decision to bring back the P3s, in July 1933, development had moved on and there would be no more easy victories for Jano's beautiful single-seaters. Already the might of the German teams – Mercedes-Benz and Auto Union – was looming on the Grand Prix horizon, and time had almost run out for the kind of engineering that had produced cars like the P3. Henceforth, power would be at a premium, newer and more sophisticated suspensions would be needed to keep more of that power on the road, and designing and developing new challengers would be more difficult, more expensive and much more time-consuming than before.

Yet the P3 was still to enjoy some moments of glory, even against such overwhelming opposition. For the time being, the German domination was less than total, and the Alfas could still pick up wins here and there, where reliability and driver skill counted for more than new ideas on the technical front. On some very rare occasions, they could win even against the full might of the German works teams, as in Tazio Nuvolari's victory in the 1935 German Grand Prix, when his bored-out 3.8-litre P3 succeeded in beating cars with a power advantage of 100 bhp and more sophisticated suspension. However, Nuvolari's brilliance and determination to beat the Germans on their own ground must have been decisive in making up for the shortcomings of what was then a rapidly ageing GP contender.

Cheaper Alfas, larger sales

On the production front, however, the rescue operation was more successful. Jano's initial design for a cheaper and simpler Alfa was a stopgap – it had to be, with time being so vital to the company's recovery. He took the 1900 version of the 1500–1750 range which had emerged as an alternative to the 2300 during 1933, and used this six-cylinder unit as the basis for a wider-bore and longer-stroke engine with a cast-iron cylinder block that had a capacity of 2309 cc, a peak power of just 68 bhp, but better torque for greater flexibility.

This return to a lazier engine could have been seen as a retrograde step in Alfa development – and the bodyweight certainly increased, in line with the bad old days. But there were two important differences: the chassis of the new car, the 6C 2300, was welded up from box sections of sheet steel instead of the old C-section girders, and its price was less than half that of the straight-8 2300. With a top speed of 120 km/h (75 mph), the car was not all that exciting: but it was commercial. In less than a year, it had sold in greater numbers than the 8C 2300 had done in four years.

The 6C 2300 followed Alfa tradition in other, more welcome ways. From a fairly pedestrian beginning, more sporting variants were soon to follow. First was the GT version with a shorter wheelbase, lighter bodywork, 76 bhp and 130 km/h (80 mph). The works team ran three tuned and rebodied versions in the 24-Hour sports car race at Pescara, where they took first three places overall. Like the Monzas before them, they were named in honour of that victory, and this additional prestige helped sales of the model range as a whole.

Eventual revisions to the range were to add hydraulic brakes and independent suspensions front and rear, but within two years the car's undoubted sales potential would be completely irrelevant. For the times were changing, and government ownership meant new priorities beyond the normal need for profitable operation. Rearmament programmes were gathering momentum, and Alfa's place in the New Order was more important as a maker of racers and aero engines than as a volume car builder for ordinary buyers.

Indeed, there was a great deal happening in the Alfa workshops during the rest of the decade. As soon as it had become obvious that the magnificent promise of the P3s had been squandered by the premature decision to withdraw them from racing at the end of the 1932 season,

spilled on the desert sand. As money dried up, fewer and fewer buyers could seriously consider a car that, whatever its undoubted virtues, cost double the price of a 1750, which itself was anything but cheap. Steadily and unmistakably, the sales figures told their own grim story: production was plummeting, income was falling with it, and while the racing programme was going from strength to strength, the production effort it depended on was running into real trouble. Unfortunately, by 1933, production was slightly less than half what the figures had been four years before.

There was only one hope for a company with a thoroughbred trade and an effective but exceedingly expensive racing programme to run: spending had to be cut, as quickly and as effectively as possible. The racing programme was brought to a sudden and complete halt. The new cars, on which so much time, effort and money had been expended, were put into storage. The company's priorities now were to find a new and much less expensive car to make, and to sell it in an increasingly bleak market place.

At the time, it must have seemed all too likely that the Alfa Romeo story could have ended then and there. In fact, rescue came swiftly if unexpectedly from the Italian government. A body called the Istituto Ricostruzione Industriale (IRI) was charged with the responsibility of taking over failing industrial companies with the objective of keeping unemployment at bay: and for Mussolini's regime, Alfa Romeo's brilliant racing record had a priceless international prestige value. So the IRI took over Alfa's assets, paid the bills and poured in extra cash to

Jano began to try and whittle away the technical lead built up by Mercedes-Benz and Auto Union. First step in the process was to design a car with a more sophisticated suspension and lower, more aerodynamic body. This was the Tipo C, which had swing-axle suspension and the 3.8-litre engine used in the last of the P3s. But the engine intended for the car was a 4-litre V12 developed from two of the classic Alfa twin-cam straight-6s harnessed together in a 60-degree V. It promised much, but the only victory it delivered was winning the Vanderbilt Cup at the Long Island Raceway in New York, with Nuvolari at the wheel: an encouraging digression, since in Europe the German cars had moved still further ahead, and something even more ambitious would be needed to defeat them.

Scuderia Ferrari had tried its own radical solution, with a car which bore the team's own badge but was an Alfa in its essentials. This was the fearsome Bimotore, which carried the twin-engine formula for instant power into a completely new area by mounting one P3 engine in front of the driver in the normal way, and fitting another one behind him. Both engines drove a centrally mounted three-speed gearbox beneath the driving seat, which then powered the rear wheels through a divided-drive arrangement as on the P3. It should have worked well enough in spite of the complexity; its frontal area and weight distribution were better than other twin-engine solutions, and the car was frighteningly fast when it ran properly, with a top speed of 320 km/h (200 mph) and enormous acceleration from more than 500 bhp in a light and compact chassis. However, the team could never cure its stupendous appetite for tyres, and the need for frequent replacements in the course of a race completely wasted the car's extra performance.

For the time being, the company, and the Italian government, would have to be content with sporting success in other areas. Jano took the chassis of the racing car, with its light, compact construction and its independent suspension, and fitted it with a 3-litre version of the old straight-8 as used in the P3. The result, clothed in sleek, carefully

streamlined bodywork, was the 8C 2900A, one of the most magnificent Alfas of all. In racing trim, this splendid car could hit a top speed of 230 km/h (143 mph). Three of the first five built were handed over to Scuderia Ferrari and entered in the 1936 Mille Miglia. They finished first, second and third; another car won the Spa 24-Hour race. Even the production six-cylinder cars took first and second place in the 1937 race, and in honour of this more spectacular success their name was changed from Pescara to Mille Miglia.

Grand Prix victories, however, were what mattered most. Next on the drawing board was a 4.5-litre version of the V12, which was fed by two superchargers and produced 430 bhp and a top speed of 306 km/h (190 mph). But power on this scale proved too much for the rear axle on the car's first outing in the 1937 Italian Grand Prix, and Jano resigned at what he, and others, saw as a personal failure. This was a loss the company could ill afford, although for some time yet it would be able to build on the foundations he had laid so securely.

As a final attempt to win the racing crown that had eluded them for so long, the Alfa engineers extended each bank of cylinders from six to a straight-8 and produced a massive V16 of just 3 litres capacity, to meet the 1938 Grand Prix requirements. With four camshafts and two

LEFT A replica of the awesome twin-engined 1935 Bimotore, developed by Scuderia Ferrari (the Alfa works team) in desperation at the continuing successes of Mercedes-Benz and Auto Union. The car's amazing appetite for tyres spoiled its otherwise promising performance.

ABOVE AND LEFT *Another of Alfa's might-have-beens, the rear-engined all-independent-suspension Tipo 512 was overtaken by the Second World War, just as the Merosi GP Alfa had been blighted by the outbreak of the First World War. The only surviving prototype stands in front of the tyre-change pit in the old paddock at Monza.*

crankshafts connected by intermediate gears, it was a complex piece of engineering and the car failed to live up to its promise: a second and a fourth place in the 1938 Italian GP were small consolation for all the expense and hard work.

Ironically, the most lasting effect of the new design was a small and simple derivative intended chiefly to give the loyal Italian crowds something to cheer about. As a break from the all-too-predictable German GP wins, the racing organizers promoted a hotly contested class of racing for voiturettes (small single-seaters with supercharged 1.5-litre engines) as curtain raisers to the main events. By fitting one of the cylinder banks and a single supercharger from the V16 into a smaller version of the all-independent-suspension racing chassis, the factory produced the Tipo 158, a car that was known by all as the Alfetta (the 'little Alfa'), and *did* begin to win races. But the real fame of these cars lay ten years away, on the other side of a world war, when they would bring the company the victories it had sought so single-mindedly.

There were other contenders being prepared in the Alfa workshops: among them the Tipo 162, which had another 3-litre V12, but with the cylinder blocks widened to an angle of 135 degrees from the 60 degrees of its predecessor, and with the connecting rods harnessed to a single common crankshaft. Then there was an even more radical design taking shape in the form of the Tipo 512, with a horizontally opposed 12-cylinder four-cam engine mounted in the rear of the car's tubular frame, and all the wheels suspended independently.

Alfa Romeo Tipo 158 Alfetta

Year made	1938
No. made	12

ENGINE

Type	In-line
No. of cylinders	8
Bore/stroke mm	58 × 70
Displacement cc	1479
Valve operation	2 rows of inclined valves in roof of combustion chamber, actuated directly by twin ohc
Sparkplugs per cyl.	1
Compression ratio	6.5:1
Induction	1 triple-choke carburettor, with twin-lobe Alfa Romeo supercharger, running at 1.32 times engine speed
BHP	195 at 7200 rpm

DRIVE TRAIN

Clutch	Multiple dry-plate
Transmission	4-speed gearbox integral with clutch and differential, rear mounted

CHASSIS

Frame	Longitudinal and transverse box sections, welded from sheet steel
Weight	620 kg (1367 lb)
Wheelbase	2500 mm (8 ft 2½ in)
Track	1250 mm (4 ft 1¼ in)
Suspension	Transverse leaf spring and swing axles
Brakes	Drums on all 4 wheels, hydraulically operated
Tyre size	6.00 × 18
Wheels	Wire, centre-lock

PERFORMANCE

Maximum speed	232 km/h (144 mph)

Alfa's most successful GP car of all, the Tipo 158, was originally a voiturette. This Alfetta, or 'little Alfa', is shown on the start line at Monza.

Luxury and performance — for a very few

The last of the prewar years saw the final flowering of the powerful, sophisticated Alfas of the 1930s in their most splendid incarnations yet. One of the half dozen straight-8 2900 A sports racing cars had been fitted with a roadgoing two-seater body which was imposing and elegant, on classic sports car lines. This attracted the company to the idea of a limited production run of a roadgoing version, still with the 2905 cc engine fed by twin superchargers, but detuned from the 220 bhp of the racing car to 180 bhp. This was the 2900 B which appeared in the short-wheelbase Corto version, basically similar to the 2900 A chassis but with a 50 mm (2 in) increase in wheelbase and a weight of 1150 kg (2530 lb). This was 300 kg (660 lb) heavier than the racer, but still good enough for a top speed of 185 km/h (115 mph) in real style. Only 20 of these magnificent cars were made, but even these were outclassed by the ten 2900 B Lungo models, with a 200 mm (8 in) longer wheelbase, a weight penalty of 100 kg (220 lb) and a top speed of 175 km/h (109 mph) with a variety of magnificent open, closed and cabriolet bodies.

BELOW *The later prewar years were to be frustrating for Alfa's racing department as its best efforts were to prove largely unsuccessful against Mercedes-Benz and Auto Union. Time after time, promising new designs like this 4.5-litre V12 of 1937 were dogged by unreliability, or were simply incapable of matching the German cars on the grounds of sheer power and acceleration.*

By this time, even the originally austere six-cylinder models had grown more ambitious. The cylinder bores were widened from 70 mm to 72 mm, to increase the capacity to 2443 cc in 1939, and the cars were now designated as the 6C 2500 range. But the philosophy was changing, too: the cars were growing bigger and more luxurious, and the introduction of Sport and Super Sport variants meant the progression as before to more sporting, more powerful, more expensive versions of the initial practical design. Unfortunately, there was the other side of the coin: production totals fell away, so that less than a hundred of the sports versions were made before the outbreak of the Second World War. It was fortunate for Alfa that normal commercial considerations had been superseded by the priorities of the aggressive and ambitious armaments programme, which saved the company from disaster in the later 1930s.

There was still a heavy price to be paid ultimately. As had been the case at the very beginning of Alfa's Grand Prix racing efforts and production success a quarter of a century before, these intriguing new designs and promising new models were soon to be overtaken by events. Once again, Europe was about to be embroiled in a world war, but this time Italy was to be involved more completely, and more disastrously, than before. By the time it was over, the country had been forced to surrender and the works had been bombed, production had stopped and the markets for cars had all but disappeared. The engineers and designers were sent away to a refuge in the Italian lakes to escape the bombing, but the factory itself, with the expensive and almost irreplaceable machine tools and production facilities, had been more than 60 per cent destroyed when the fighting ceased and peace returned. Even the brave new plans made during the wartime years for a return to mass-market production were completely impossible in the light of the destruction. This time it seemed as if the company had no real future at all.

Alfa Romeo 8C 2900 B Lungo
Years made 1937–9
No. made 10

ENGINE		CHASSIS	
Type	In-line	**Frame**	Longitudinal and transverse box sections, welded from sheet steel
No. of cylinders	8		
Bore/stroke mm	68 × 100		
Displacement cc	2905		
Valve operation	2 rows of inclined valves in roof of combustion chambers, directly actuated by twin overhead camshafts	**Weight**	1250 kg (2750 lb)
		Wheelbase	3000 mm (9 ft 10 in)
		Track	1350 mm (4 ft 5 in)
		Suspension – front	Independent, with coil springs
Sparkplugs per cyl.	1	**Suspension – rear**	Independent, with transverse leaf spring and telescopic shock absorbers
Compression ratio	5.75:1		
Induction	2 downdraught carburettors and 2 twin-lobe superchargers, running at 1.448 times engine speed		
		Brakes	Drums on all 4 wheels, hydraulically operated
BHP	180 at 5200 rpm	**Tyre size**	5.50 × 19
		Wheels	Wire, centre-lock

DRIVE TRAIN		PERFORMANCE	
Clutch	Multiple dry-plate	**Maximum speed**	175 km/h (110 mph)
Transmission	4-speed manual gearbox		

LEFT *Saved from bankruptcy by government takeover, Alfa was increasingly expected to earn prestige for the State: by building aero engines, by winning races, and by using the small amount of spare production capacity to turn out a few exotic cars. Only ten of the long-chassis versions of the 1938 8C 2900 B were made.*

Wartime Ruin and Postwar Recovery

As peace came to battered Europe, the position of Alfa's workers and the company they worked for seemed equally desperate. The labour force had expanded several times over to meet the swelling demand for aero engines which had made the Portello works such a priority target for Allied bombers, and now the company was expressly forbidden to make any more war materials. All that was left was car production, but without parts and without working machinery that seemed a forlorn hope indeed.

In fact, Alfa's workforce was to be its salvation – in two ways. The workers themselves knew all too well that the company's continued existence would mean their own survival in the postwar world, with all their hopes of employment and eventual prosperity. And the Italian government had even more urgent reasons to keep Alfa Romeo operating, rather than swell the ranks of the unemployed even further. So everyone wanted the company to survive, but that depended on being able to turn out cars while the factory and the machinery on which mass-production depended were put back into working order.

So it was that history repeated itself: just as the Alfas of 1919 and 1920 were made from parts produced in 1913 and 1914, so those of 1946 and 1947 were remakes of the Alfas of 1939. Or some of them at least: for while the prestige production had been concentrated on the splendid 8C 2900 Bs, that small but steady turnout of 6C 2500 models had been maintained in touring, sport and Super Sport variants right up to the outbreak of war, and even afterwards, whenever time and effort could be diverted to them.

Fortunately there were parts in plenty for these models, and they needed relatively little machinery to assemble them. All that could be done to update them was to change details like the gearchange – shifted from the floor to the more fashionable position on the steering column – and the rating of the rear shock absorbers. In all other respects, the first production cars were all too recognizably prewar models.

However, the undemanding postwar market wanted cars, almost any cars, and the 6C 2500s sold as fast as they could leave the factory. All the same, the demand for sporting Alfas was still very much alive, and more sporting versions were sold than the standard touring cars. In fact, so loyal was this market that the first step towards a new model was taken by fitting a revised body design to the existing mechanicals. With smooth streamlining, and a rakishly curved fastback tail, the new version looked a great deal more modern than its predecessors and it was given a name to symbolize this break from the past. They called it the Freccia d'Oro ('Golden Arrow'), and it was a brilliant commercial success by the standards of the time.

But all the updated prewar models, however popular, were palliatives rather than cures for what ailed the company. As the recovery continued, Alfa's future was clearly marked out. With all the unused factory space and all the extra workers provided for prewar armaments production, the only way all these resources could be properly employed was by expanding production beyond all previous limits. And that could only be done with a design intended from the beginning for this type of operation, and this kind of market.

Mass production and a new design

The answer to these exacting requirements was to be an entirely new car, the first of the modern Alfa Romeos in its philosophy, its engineering and its character. There were, it was true, some features inherited from past designs, like the use of an engine with hemispherical combustion chambers, inclined overhead valves and twin overhead camshafts, but in most other respects the new car broke completely new ground.

Jano had left the company a decade before, but Alfa had been fortunate indeed to find a worthy successor in the shape of Dr Orazio Satta Puliga, generally known as Satta. His inspiration shaped the company's efforts till his death in 1973, and his memory is still revered in the company he served so well. In 1949 he was just 37 years old, and was facing a challenge that might have daunted an engineer with three times his professional experience. Yet his touch was sure and his

PREVIOUS PAGES *Postwar conditions made Alfa Romeo a mass producer: but that did not mean the cars could not be elegant, and exciting. When the Giulietta, the first really mass-market Alfa, appeared in 1954, it was this sleek Sprint version that emerged first.*

thinking logical, original and effective. Alfa Romeo, at the moment of its greatest need, had once again found the man for the job.

Within the basic limits of the configuration used by Jano before him, Satta set out to produce an engine that would run faster and develop more power from a given size: this meant wider bores and a shorter stroke, to keep stresses within bounds. But careful balancing meant that a four-cylinder engine could be as smooth and efficient as a prewar six, with a reduction in moving parts and cost, and a corresponding improvement in reliability.

Of course, this new thinking produced problems – valve cooling for example. But Alfa's engineers had not been aero engine builders for nothing, and they adopted the solution they had developed for the much fiercer conditions that applied in aircraft power units: chrome-plated valve stems with an inner sodium core for more efficient cooling, and valve seats in stellite alloy set into the light-alloy cylinder head. The cylinder block, unlike those on the prewar engines, was of cast iron but the sump, instead of also being cast, was actually welded up from sheet steel for lightness and simplicity.

The biggest change in the new model, however, was in the chassis rather than the power unit. Gone for ever was the old ladder-frame chassis of the original Alfas, or for that matter the welded box-section frame of more recent cars. The 1900, as the new car was designated, from its original engine capacity of 1884 cc, was not only the first truly mass-produced Alfa. It was also the first to have a monocoque body–chassis combination, where the body itself, suitably strength-

LEFT *Alfa was always fortunate in finding the right man at the right time to produce its cars. In the postwar years, it was Satta – Orazio Satta Puliga – who was responsible for designs ranging from the 1900 to the production Alfettas of the 1970s.*

RIGHT *Alfa's first postwar cars were assembled from stocks of parts for the prewar 6C 2500. This one was fitted with bodywork by Touring, to produce the imposing 1950 Villa d'Este coupé.*

ened and reinforced where necessary, carried all the stresses without depending on a separate chassis frame. This was inevitable, in spite of the extra complexity of the design, given Satta's insistence on a car that should be a genuine four-seater, yet had to be light enough to provide a real performance from the 90 bhp of the original version of the 1900 engine. And the car's performance was going to be the chief, if not the only, attraction to enthusiast buyers. Again in the interests of saving both weight and cost, the interior was austere indeed compared with the luxury of prewar Alfas; and the car's lines seemed to have been drawn with visual excitement or interest as a last priority.

There was one other backward step in the new design – or so it appeared at first glance. Prewar models had inherited the all-round independent suspension of the later racing cars, but the 1900 went back to a rigid rear axle layout, for the soundest of reasons. A properly set-up rear suspension tended to be heavy, complex and expensive, and one that was not correctly set up was worse than useless. Better by far, reasoned Satta, to go for the lightness and simplicity of a solid rear axle, but to take the utmost care to support and locate it properly, so that it behaved itself efficiently and predictably, with no trace of problems like axle hop under severe cornering loads on bumpy surfaces.

The resulting system was one that Alfa was to use for another 20 years: the axle itself was hung on coil springs and trailing arms, but the differential gearbox was actually mounted on the chassis itself, to prevent sideways movement and reduce unsprung weight. This was combined with independent suspension at the front end of the car, provided by coil springs and double wishbones, which gave the car agile handling and utter predictability under a wide range of cornering

conditions, so that even the less skilful drivers could make full use of its performance on twisting and badly maintained roads.

Slowly but surely to success

All in all, the car represented so many breaks with tradition that it was a commercial leap in the dark in a still hesitant postwar market. And although the 1900 was designed for mass production from the beginning, the factory was still less than adequately equipped to turn the car out in the planned volume. To begin with, extra workers had to make up for missing machinery by carrying out operations by hand, so output began at a low level and crept up slowly, imperceptibly but steadily.

For all the differences the 1900's design presented when compared with its prewar stablemates, it was still every bit an Alfa in its philosophy and behaviour, and it was noticeable that every car finished was being snapped up by eager buyers. As production climbed, so did sales, and before long the company was able to add more sporting variations to the range, in the time-honoured Alfa manner. The 1900's first public showing was at Turin in May 1950, and the following year a version called the TI (for Turismo Internazionale, a keenly contested category in Italian racing at that time) with bigger valves, higher compression and a double-choke carburettor to boost the power to 100 bhp and the top speed from 150 km/h (93 mph) to 170 km/h (106 mph), was unveiled to an increasingly eager public.

The bodywork of the 1900TI was closely similar to the ordinary saloon: the intention was to perpetuate the wolf-in-sheep's-clothing appeal of a car that looked pedestrian but delivered exhilarating performance, that was closely in tune with the spirit of the time. However, there were still buyers who wanted more sporting looks, so that two other versions of the 1900 made their appearance in 1951. By shortening the wheelbase and cutting the weight, Alfa was able to provide the cream of Italy's independent coachbuilders with a frame on which to hang coupé or cabriolet bodywork. Thus Pininfarina designed an open-top cabriolet with a top speed of 170 km/h (106 mph) with the TI engine, while Touring's more streamlined closed coupé could manage 182 km/h (113 mph).

These more elegant versions were but the icing on the cake; they accounted between them for about ten per cent of total sales, as they were considerably more expensive than the basic 1900 or even the standard-bodied TI. But their very existence was a reminder that Alfas were still worthy of such expensive cosmetic treatment, and even the thrifty buyers of the 1900 knew full well the engineering under the panelling was still the same. Then, even as 1900 production began to soar far beyond any levels attained by the most popular of its predecessors, plans were already being drawn up for its successors. For the time being, the engine size was increased to 1975 cc in 1953 and the various models, the 1900 Berlina, TI and Sprint, were given an extra 'Super'

tag to denote the increase in capacity and performance.

Given the long-term success of the 1900, it was already clear that another recurring theme in the Alfa story was bound to make itself apparent yet again. On two previous occasions, the fast, powerful and luxurious sporting cars that were the basis of the company's fame had been dropped because the market was languishing under an economic recession. On each occasion, they were replaced by more prosaic and less sophisticated successors. These new cars had then gone on to respond to market recovery by growing more ambitious, more sporting, more lavishly equipped, until eventually there was little to distinguish them from their immediate predecessors.

In a sense, the 1900 was a third attempt by the company to respond to altered conditions, although in this case the changes in the market, and

in the car that was evolved to meet them, turned out to be particularly radical. The 1900 was like no earlier Alfa in anything save its name and its basic philosophy: but in one way it was about to follow family tradition by paving the way for a more glamorous and more identifiable successor. The 1900 may have looked more like a Fiat than an Alfa, as one of the design team put it, but its replacement would cause no such confusion over its true identity.

Romeo and Giulietta

This replacement was taking shape during a period when, early in the 1950s, the Italian recovery was making it possible to go several steps further towards truly efficient mass production. The 1900 had filled the bill splendidly in seeing the company through the transition from

BELOW AND RIGHT *The 1900 broke new ground for Alfa in two respects: it was the first Alfa with a combined body–chassis unit, and it was built in greater numbers than any previous model. In other respects it was like all other Alfas: the 1900TI appeared regularly in races like the 1954 Mille Miglia.*

Alfa Romeo 1900	
Years made	1950–3
No. made	7611
ENGINE	
Type	In-line
No. of cylinders	4
Bore/stroke mm	82.55 × 88
Displacement cc	1884
Valve operation	2 rows of inclined valves in roof of combustion chambers, actuated directly by twin overhead camshafts
Sparkplugs per cyl.	1
Compression ratio	7.5 : 1
Induction	Single carburettor
BHP	90 at 5200 rpm
DRIVE TRAIN	
Clutch	Single dry-plate
Transmission	4-speed manual and two-stage propeller shaft to rear-mounted differential
CHASSIS	
Frame	Monocoque body–chassis unit
Weight	1100 kg (2425 lb)
Wheelbase	2630 mm (8 ft 7½ in)
Track – front	1320 mm (4 ft 4 in)
Track – rear	1325 mm (4 ft 4¼ in)
Suspension – front	Independent, with coil springs and double wishbones
Suspension – rear	Solid rear axle, with coil springs, trailing arms and triangular locating member
Brakes	Drums on all 4 wheels, hydraulically operated
Tyre size	165 × 400
Wheels	Pressed-steel disc
PERFORMANCE	
Maximum speed	150 km/h (93 mph)

LEFT *The Disco Volante of 1952 was based on mechanical parts from the 1900 series and was designed with competition in mind. But it never raced, and remains famous for its unusual lines rather than its sporting prowess. Three versions were made, two open cars and this closed sports coupé.*

RIGHT *More successful, in competition terms, was the 6C 3000 CM, based on a projected six-cylinder 3-litre version of the 1900 engine, and fitted into a modified version of the 6C 2500 chassis. A closed coupé example of the car finished second in the 1953 Mille Miglia. This open version, driven by Fangio, won the Supercortemaggiore GP in 1954.*

RIGHT *This view of the Disco Volante on test shows one of the two open versions, with the sharp-edged bodywork that gave the car its 'Flying Saucer' name. The other open car had normal body panelling.*

BELOW *Final proof that postwar requirements had not killed off Alfa's traditions came with the introduction of the Giulietta Spider. a classic open two-seater with bodywork by Pininfarina, which appeared in early 1955.*

prewar quality to postwar volume production, but in engineering terms it was already dated. It was too large in its overall size, it was too heavy and, for the same reason, its engine was too big when many countries taxed their cars on the basis of engine capacity. It was also too expensive for export markets: and to expand production still further, it was essential to produce a smaller, cheaper, more attractive model to appeal to buyers abroad as much as to the loyal customers in Italy.

The new car therefore started off both shorter and narrower than the 1900: the wheelbase was trimmed by 250 mm (10 in), and the track narrowed by 37 mm (1½ in) at the front and 50 mm (2 in) at the back. But the carefully shaped body not only allowed room for four passengers (or five at a squash), it gave them better visibility through larger windows and narrower screen pillars and, so far had monocoque body-chassis design advanced in five years, it achieved both of these

benefits while cutting the total weight of the car from 1100 kg (2425 lb) to 900 kg (1984 lb).

To be fair, some of this weight reduction was achieved in the design of the engine: the cylinder block was cast in light alloy, like those of the prewar Alfas, and the usual hemispherical combustion chambers, inclined valves and twin overhead camshafts followed the customary formula. The dimensions, however, were new: with the bores at 74 mm and the stroke at 75 mm, this little four-cylinder unit had a capacity of only 1290 cc. With a single carburettor, this was enough to produce 53 bhp, which left it some way short of the 1900 in power-to-weight ratio, but the almost square bore-to-stroke ratio of the engine made it a promising candidate for further development.

The result of all this careful design work was one of the most famous, and best-loved, Alfas of all: the Giulietta. Like the 1900 before it, this was to be not a single model, but a range of different versions based on the same mechanical design. It was also highly significant, in terms of Alfa's intended policy, that the first version to reach the public gaze was not the basic saloon, elegant and attractive though that was, but the sleeker and more sporting closed coupé called the Giulietta Sprint.

This had a slightly lighter and much shapelier body, designed by Bertone as a two-plus-two of unashamedly sporting appearance. It also had a twin-choke carburettor and higher-compression version of the engine which delivered 80 bhp and propelled the car to a top speed of 165 km/h (103 mph). Its most significant virtue, however, was its price. Not only did it sell on the home market for the equivalent of £1000, but this placed it at just over half the cost of its 1900 equivalent, the only slightly faster 1900 Super Sprint. The saloon was cheaper still – just under £800 on the Italian market, although the performance was slightly less exciting.

The Alfa people themselves were convinced that the way the car responded, to the throttle and the steering, was immeasurably more important than styling, so they clothed it in a body that was neutral and slightly unfashionable by the standards of its time. Paradoxically, this means the original Giulietta looks more modern now than many of its competitors of the mid-1950s.

The Giulietta Sprint appeared late in 1954, the saloon in the following spring. In the summer of 1955 came the third model in the range, which marked a further nod to well-established Alfa traditions: the open two-seat Giulietta Spider, with an elegant Pininfarina body, and modern refinements like wind-up windows and an easy-to-fold hood. The Spider shared the higher-performance version of the 1290 cc engine used by the coupé, and it was slightly lighter still, so that improved performance was another of its attractions. Like the Sprint it had circular instruments, including a rev counter, to replace the basic strip speedometer of the saloon, and the gearchange was back where it belonged, in the view of every sports car driver, controlled by a neat and beautifully precise floor-mounted lever.

If the 1900 broke new ground in terms of production figures for Alfa, the Giulietta took the theme much further. More than 16,000 Giulietta saloons were made in less than three years, and even the more specialized sporting versions sold almost as well. By 1961, more than 14,000 Spiders alone had been sold, which would have seemed inconceivable by prewar standards for a sporting two-seater.

However, this was eclipsed by the sales of the most successful Giulietta version of all, which was to set the pattern for each subsequent model range. This appeared three years after the original introduction, and was arrived at by the fairly logical step of putting the higher-performance engine of the Sprint and Spider into the saloon

body, to provide sporting performance with passenger room and a low price tag. The result was the Giulietta TI, which sold for just £85 more than the standard saloon and had a top speed of 150 km/h (93 mph). The combination proved irresistible, and although the model appeared so late in the story, by the time it was replaced in 1965 more TIs had been made and sold than all the other Giulietta models put together.

Racing hopes revived

The continuing success of the 1900s and the Giuliettas in commercial terms had brought a new stability to the company after the challenges and problems of the immediate prewar and postwar years. During the early 1950s, the Technical Department had produced a number of interesting projects to keep the Alfa Romeo name alive in a motor sport context, to remind a new generation of owners and buyers of the marque's capabilities. First of these, in 1952, had been a racing version of the 1900 which showed no resemblance to its parent at all. At the time the first sightings of UFOs, or flying saucers, had been in the news, and the new design was christened the Disco Volante because of its futuristic and distinctive body shape.

The thinking behind the design was clear enough. The cylinder bores of the 1900 engine were widened to 85 mm. This took the capacity to 1997.4 cc, which was about as close as it was safe to go in entering the 2-litre racing class. With higher compression, at 8.73 to 1, and two double-choke carburettors and racing camshaft settings, the engine was able to deliver 158 bhp, compared with 100 bhp for the slightly smaller production version. This was fitted into a new racing body with a carefully shaped undertray, and upperworks that were intended to cut drag, as well as weight, to the minimum. Three cars were built, an open two-seater and a closed coupé, both with the sharp-edged side panelling that accounted for the car's name, and an open hillclimb version with more conventionally shaped sides.

The car's top speed was a competitive 217 km/h (135 mph), but ultimately the Disco Volante failed to live up to its promise. Part of the problem was that the careful attention to aerodynamics was counter-productive: in trying to cut drag to the minimum, the engineers induced lift at the rear end of the car, which made it difficult to handle. This, added to the inevitable problems of consistency and reliability that are inseparable from any new racing car, made the Disco Volante another name on Alfa's list of might-have-beens. However, the name itself was to be brought out of cold storage and applied to a non-racing version of another car altogether, a design that did have some sporting success to its credit.

This was the 6C 3000 CM and it owed its origins to an Alfa project for a six-cylinder version of the 1900 engine which could have been used for a small-volume luxury model. The result of this was an engine with the same 82.55 mm bores as the 1900 (the odd measurement was due to the use of British Hepolite pistons, these being the only suitable components available in Italy at the time) and a slightly longer stroke at 92 mm, producing a capacity of 2955 cc. After the six-cylinder production car project was dropped, the engine was fitted with three twin-choke carburettors and higher compression to boost its power from 120 bhp to 168 bhp, and fitted into a competition coupé that had originally been built around one of the old 6C 2500 engines.

This first racing version of the 6C 2500 was entered in the 1950 Mille Miglia, without success. Later versions of the car had an 87 mm bore, 98 mm stroke, 3495 cc version of the engine delivering up to 275 bhp, and one of these finished second in the 1953 race. Another shorter and lighter version was built and fitted with the original 3-litre size engine – this was called the 6C 3000 PR (for *passo ridotto*, or shortened wheelbase) – but it crashed on test at Monza. Another example was built with the sharp-edged body panelling of the Disco Volante, and was also sometimes known by this name, which may account for the racing success of the six-cylinder car being wrongly credited to the smaller 1900 Disco Volante.

Filling the gaps

In the meantime, back on the production front, the Giulietta range was suffering from only one real problem. In moving further down the market to increase production above the level of the 1900s, Alfa had left a gap in the large-car sector which might otherwise have been filled by the six-cylinder version of the 1900 – this had instead given birth to

Alfa Romeo Giulietta Sprint Speciale

Years made 1957–62
No. made 1366

ENGINE

Type	In-line
No. of cylinders	4
Bore/stroke mm	74 × 75
Displacement cc	1290
Valve operation	2 rows of inclined valves in roof of combustion chambers, actuated directly by twin overhead camshafts
Sparkplugs per cyl.	1
Compression ratio	9.7:1
Induction	2 horizontal twin-choke carburettors
BHP	100 at 6500 rpm

DRIVE TRAIN

Clutch	Single dry-plate
Transmission	5-speed manual gearbox and propeller shaft to rear axle

CHASSIS

Frame	Monocoque body–chassis unit
Weight	860 kg (1892 lb)
Wheelbase	2250 mm (7 ft 5½ in)
Track – front	1292 mm (4 ft 3 in)
Track – rear	1270 mm (4 ft 2 in)
Suspension – front	Independent, with coil springs and double wishbones
Suspension – rear	Solid rear axle, with coil springs, trailing arms and triangular locating member
Brakes	Drums, with three shoes on all 4 wheels, hydraulically operated (last 30 cars produced had discs on front wheels only)
Tyre size	155 × 15
Wheels	Pressed-steel disc

PERFORMANCE

Maximum speed	200 km/h (125 mph)

In the eyes of many enthusiasts, Bertone's impeccable Giulietta Sprint Speciale was the most beautiful Alfa of all time. Built on a racing variant of the Giulietta chassis, it was to be followed by a similar version of the Giulia. Provided by Lincoln Small.

the 3000 CM racing cars. There had been a stopgap in the form of a series of larger-bodied cars which used the 1975 cc 1900 Super power unit, but had been called, rather confusingly, the 2000 range since the introduction of the Giulietta. Not until 1962 did Alfa produce big six-cylinder cars, the 2600s, which used the body designs of the square-cut 2000 saloon, the open two-seat Pininfarina Spider and the Bertone Sprint Coupé (the last two bearing an amazing family resemblance to their smaller Giulietta equivalents), but fitted with an 83 mm bore, 79.6 mm stroke, 2584 cc version of the classic twin-cam engine delivering 145 bhp. The Sprint was an especially handsome car, but for some reason these admittedly costly models never achieved real success in sales terms, although they remain popular with collectors.

Another small-volume car appeared during the late 1950s, this time based on the Giulietta, which has been even more popular with Alfa enthusiasts ever since. This was the beautiful Bertone-bodied Giulietta Sprint Speciale, or SS, with a shorter wheelbase than the standard Giulietta Sprint and a more powerful 100 bhp version of the engine, which gave it a top speed of 200 km/h (125 mph): in other words, it was fast as well as beautiful, to the extent that many owners were able to use the car in racing to some effect.

Finally, at about the time when Alfa was going back into the big-car market with the six-cylinder 2600s, the company was also toying with the idea of moving into the small-car market as well – a possibility on most motor manufacturers' minds after the amazing success of the British Mini. Alfa built a small-car prototype called the Tipo 103 which featured the smallest version of the twin-cam engine ever built: with 66 mm bores and a 66.5 mm stroke, it had a capacity of 896 cc and, with a single carburettor, delivered 52 bhp. It was fitted into a compact, square-cut body like a half-scale replica of the 2000 Berlina, but arranged to drive the front wheels through a four-speed gearbox. Coil-spring independent suspension and disc brakes on all four wheels, and an all-up weight of 725 kg (1600 lb) promised reasonable performance, and the top speed was 130 km/h (80 mph). Three engines and a single car were made in 1960 and 1961, but the project was shelved because of the higher priority of the Giulietta's successor. When eventually the smallest Alfa of all was put into production it was in a completely different form.

Giulias and Alfettas

At the time of its introduction, the Giulietta had hit the market right where it was most needed. The price, the size, the power and the performance had been what buyers were looking for, and the car's commercial success reflected that fact. But by the early 1960s the competition had caught up, and it was clear that public taste was calling for more power, more performance and more excitement from its successor. So work began on the Giulietta's bigger sister called, appropriately enough, the Giulia.

From the very beginning the resemblance went further than just the similarity in name. The Giulia engine was still the twin-overhead camshaft four that had been used in the 1900 and the Giulietta. This time, however, the bores were set at 78 mm and the stroke at 82 mm, which produced a capacity of 1570 cc: the Giulietta's 1290 cc had been well placed for racing versions to be competitive in the 1300 cc racing classes, and similarly the Giulia should fit equally well into the 1600 category.

Two of the models would have the new engine, and the five-speed gearbox, in the same bodies as used for the Giulietta. These were the Spider and Sprint, although here too changes were on the way eventually. But the Giulia saloon was completely redesigned, and once again a sporting version was first to appear, in June 1962, as the Giulia TI. Oddly enough, if this version of the car did have a family resemblance, it was to the little Tipo 103 front-wheel-drive mini-Alfa prototype, with its simple, unembellished but oddly effective boxy shape, rather than to its more curvaceous predecessor. It was apparently the personal insistence of its designer, Satta, on the style that determined its shape and identity. Subsequent wind-tunnel testing helped to produce a body that was reasonably efficient aerodynamically as well as one that was impossible to confuse with any other car whatsoever. In its original form, the Giulia TI delivered 92 bhp and was capable of 165 km/h (103 mph), with the Sprint and Spider another 7 km/h (4½ mph) above this figure.

Under the skin, the mechanical design was much the same, save for refinements like the five-speed gearbox, a light-alloy differential case, and a revised way of locating the differential and preventing sideways movement under cornering loads. All these had been introduced as part of a set of detailed but worthwhile improvements, and over the decade and more following the Giulia's appearance the range was to grow and mature and evolve, with a series of additions to and variations and replacements of the basic three-model line-up. Indeed, for a time after the appearance of the Giulia, the production of the Giulietta TI continued. Even after the range was terminated, the Giulietta unit survived and was used to power a set of smaller-engined derivatives of the Giulia range.

Another of the Giuliettas to be transformed into a Giulia equivalent was Bertone's Sprint Speciale – in fact slightly more Giulia SSs were made than Giulietta SSs. As before, the car had a more powerful version of the standard engine, delivering 112 bhp, and in 1963 this unit was put into the Giulia saloon to produce the Giulia TI Super. At the same time, a modified Sprint with more room for rear passengers,

called the Giulia Sprint GT, appeared. A year later a Giulietta-engined version of this model, now called simply the 1300 Sprint, added to the options open to sporting-minded buyers.

So the story went on: in the summer of 1964, the Giulia saloon was fitted with a more powerful version of the Giulietta TI engine to produce the Giulia 1300 Berlina, with a top speed of 160 km/h (100 mph). As the Giulia saloon range now had a TI and a TI Super, the third variation, added in 1965, had a medium-tune, 98-102 bhp version of the engine, with a more sporting trim (wooden dash, circular instruments, improved seats and wood-rim steering wheel) and, logically but confusingly, it became the Giulia Super.

Then in 1966, the 82 bhp, 160 km/h (100 mph) Giulia 1300 TI appeared, together with the redesigned Spider (later to be called the Duetto) which shared its 109 bhp engine with the higher-performance version of the Sprint, now renamed the Sprint GT Veloce, or GTV for short. In the autumn a smaller-engined version of the GTV appeared as the GT 1300 Junior, followed two years later by the Spider 1300, which had the same Pininfarina bodywork as its 1600 stablemate. To the eyes of many Alfa fans, these new two-seaters lacked the elegance and balance of the earlier Pininfarina design produced originally as the Giulietta Spider, but in time they became deservedly popular. The looks improved when the original rounded tail was replaced by a more vertically chopped-off Kamm variant, and in time this was to be the most long-lived of all the Giulia range, soldiering on with larger engines into the mid-1980s.

The Giulias as such lasted until 1972, although their replacements made their appearance early in 1968. In most respects, these were simply larger-engined replacements; however, the styling of the Berlina was tidied up by Bertone and the entire range (now that the engine capacity was increased to 1779 cc) was given the nostalgic title of the '1750'. The Berlina now had a top speed of better than 180 km/h (112 mph), and the more sporting variants could manage 190 km/h (120 mph). Four years later, with the dropping of the 'Giulia' name (the model survived, as did the Giulietta, with a numerical identification – in this case as the various 1600 models), the 1750s were themselves replaced by the 2000 series. These had a wider-bore version of the engine delivering 132 bhp in all three models: top speed of the saloon

PREVIOUS PAGES *Successor to the excellent Giulia GTZ Tubolare, the 1965 TZ2 was to spearhead Autodelta's efforts in every kind of competition from sprints to endurance races, until emphasis shifted to the GTA (see photograph on page 56).*

ABOVE RIGHT *With one exception, the various models in the Giulia line-up were very similar to their predecessors: compare this picture of the 1962 Giulia Sprint with the 1954 Giulietta Sprint on pages 40–1.*

BELOW AND RIGHT *And this was the exception: the boxy shape of the Giulia saloon in its various forms (Normale, TI, Super and TI Super) was to become familiar over more than a decade of production. This is a 1972 Giulia Super, which appeared ten years after the original.*

Alfa Romeo Giulia Super
Years made	1965–72
No. made	12,459

ENGINE
Type	In-line
No. of cylinders	4
Bore/stroke mm	78 × 82
Displacement cc	1570
Valve operation	2 rows of inclined valves in roof of combustion chambers, actuated directly by twin overhead camshafts
Sparkplugs per cyl.	1
Compression ratio	9:1
Induction	2 horizontal twin-choke carburettors
BHP	102 at 5500 rpm

DRIVE TRAIN
Clutch	Single dry-plate
Transmission	5-speed manual

CHASSIS
Frame	Monocoque body–chassis unit
Weight	990 kg (2183 lb)
Wheelbase	2510 mm (8 ft 3 in)
Track – front	1324 mm (4 ft 4 in)
Track – rear	1274 mm (4 ft 2¼ in)
Suspension – front	Independent, with coil springs and double wishbones
Suspension – rear	Solid rear axle, with coil springs, trailing arms and triangular locating member
Brakes	Servo-assisted discs on all 4 wheels
Tyre size	155 SR 15
Wheels	Pressed-steel disc

PERFORMANCE
Maximum speed	175 km/h (109 mph) +

RIGHT *The racing version of the Giulia Sprint GT was designated the GTA. Here (Brno, 1970) a larger capacity version, the GTAm, shows off its cornering ability on three wheels at the hands of Dutchman Toine Hezemans, who won a European Championship for Alfa.*

BELOW *The production equivalent of the GTA was the Giulia GTV, which was eventually developed into this 2-litre 2000 GTV, a highly desirable combination of looks, comfort, character and performance popular with collectors. Provided by Barry Coupe.*

was 190 km/h (120 mph), and that of the coupé and spider just 5 km/h (3 mph) more.

These were the final flowerings of the Giulia range – the 2000 Spider is still in the current line-up – but by this time they had been joined by another strain of production Alfas. Their name, and some of their basic engineering, is of a different derivation, altogether: from prewar Alfas rather than postwar designs, and from Grand Prix single-seaters rather than production saloons.

A famous name revived

One of the few breaks in the gloom of Alfa's racing history in the last prewar years had been provided by a car that was itself an offshoot of one of the promising, but ultimately disappointing, designs developed to challenge the German domination of Grand Prix events. In 1938 the old free-formula regulations, which had allowed the development of ever bigger and more powerful engines, had been replaced by a 3-litre capacity limit, which should in theory have allowed all the Grand Prix

contenders a fresh start under this new set of rules.

In fact, the Germans proved to be better prepared than anyone, perhaps because of the enormous sums available from their government to finance radical new developments to suit the changing formula. Alfa for its part had developed a 3-litre V16, the Tipo 316. But, as we have seen, there was another string to the team's bow in the shape of a voiturette racer to compete under a 1.5-litre capacity limit. It used half the GP engine, a supercharged twin-cam straight-8 of 1479 cc, producing a creditable 195 to 225 bhp in a car that weighed 620 kg (1367 lb), substantially less than the GP car. In this hotly contested class of racing, Alfa won a succession of victories in the last two seasons before the war: but the greatest days of the Alfettas, the 'little Alfas', still lay ahead.

Once motor racing restarted after the Second World War, two major changes had occurred. The German teams had vanished, for the time being, and the regulations had changed to an option of 4.5-litre engines without superchargers, or 1.5 litres with superchargers, a formula that

RIGHT *For all the company's postwar preoccupation with mass production, it was still possible for Alfa buyers to find small-volume, individual designs from bodybuilders like Zagato. This 1972 Giulia-based 1600 Junior Z was provided by Roger Peirson.*

**Alfa Romeo
1600 Spider (Duetto)**
Years made 1966–7

ENGINE

Type	In-line
No. of cylinders	4
Bore/stroke mm	78 × 82
Displacement cc	1570
Valve operation	2 rows of inclined valves in roof of combustion chambers, actuated directly by twin overhead camshafts
Sparkplugs per cyl.	1
Compression ratio	9:1
Induction	2 horizontal twin-choke carburettors
BHP	109 at 6000 rpm

DRIVE TRAIN

Clutch	Single dry-plate
Transmission	5-speed manual gearbox, propeller shaft to rear axle

CHASSIS

Frame	Monocoque body–chassis unit
Weight	990 kg (2167 lb)
Wheelbase	2250 mm (7 ft 5½ in)
Track – front	1310 mm (4 ft 3½ in)
Track – rear	1270 mm (4 ft 2 in)
Suspension – front	Independent, with coil springs and double wishbones
Suspension – rear	Solid rear axle, with coil springs, trailing arms and triangular locating member
Brakes	Discs on all 4 wheels, hydraulically operated
Tyre size	155 × 15
Wheels	Pressed-steel disc

PERFORMANCE

Maximum speed	185 km/h (115 mph) +

Everyone's idea of what driving an Alfa ought to be like: the 1600 Spider Duetto. Provided by Barry Coupe.

could have been designed with the Alfettas in mind. It was just as well: with all the problems of restarting production and developing new cars, designing and building a new Grand Prix racer would have been quite out of the question.

Even so, there were problems: the prewar Alfettas had given their transmissions a hard time, and since then the switch to higher-pressure supercharging and other improvements had boosted the power to 275 bhp. In their first appearance after the war, a race at St-Cloud, just outside Paris, two Alfettas broke down with transmission trouble – and these were the original, less powerful models. But although the problem took time to cure completely, Alfa managed to field stronger and stronger teams to win the other three races in which they were entered during that 1946 season. In 1947, they did even better: every race they entered was won convincingly by drivers of the calibre of Achille Varzi, Count Carlo Felice Trossi, Jean-Pierre Wimille and Consalvo Sanesi, against very spirited opposition from Maserati in particular.

By 1948, still higher blower pressures had pushed the power to 310 bhp, at the expense of correspondingly higher stresses. Again the Alfettas triumphed, with wins in all the events they entered; one significant factor, however, was the appearance of the first Ferraris, produced by Alfa's former racing manager, as a new, and ultimately much more formidable challenge.

In 1949, faced with a shortage of drivers and the need for more development on the cars, Alfa withdrew from Grand Prix racing. The company returned in 1950 to win again, in every race in which it entered cars. But the Ferrari challenge was growing: after following Alfa down the 1.5-litre supercharged route, Ferrari had now opted for a much more successful unblown 4.5-litre engine. However, his cars were plagued with handling problems from their swing-axle suspensions and until a new design, based on the same de Dion axle used on the Alfettas, was ready, the cars were unable to make full use of their performance.

In 1951 Ferrari represented a much more formidable threat: by this time, the Alfettas were delivering 425 bhp at 9300 rpm, at the expense of a range of only a mile and a half on each gallon, which was a real handicap on the longer-distance races. They won, narrowly, in the Swiss, the Belgian and in the French GPs, chased home by the Ferraris in each case; but it was the opposition that triumphed in the British and German GPs and, worst of all, in the Italian GP at Monza. Only by a resounding win in the Spanish GP (where the Ferraris fitted larger tyres in an attempt to cut pitstops and this stratagem misfired) was Alfa able to win its fourth season's racing in five years, and cars already more than 13 years old were wheeled away into honoured retirement.

As an achievement, it was magnificent, and in one short period it made up for much of the prewar frustration and disappointment. Ever since then the name Alfetta has had special significance for Alfa Romeo and the marque's most loyal followers, and it was hardly surprising when, more than 20 years later, such a hallowed name reappeared in a very different guise on a new range of production cars.

There was more in this than mere nostalgia. By the 1970s the basic design of the engine, chassis and suspension, which was still essentially that produced for the 1900s of 20 years before, was beginning to show its age. Alfa's competitors had covered a lot of ground in that time, and production cars had far better roadholding than had been the case when the 1900's suspension was designed. So it was time for new thinking: independent rear suspension was an obvious need, but as before, the system would have to be set up properly to be worth while.

In the end, the Alfa engineers did a great deal more than revise the rear suspension for the new model that was ultimately to take over from the Giulia and its immediate successors. They looked at the whole question of weight distribution, which has such an effect on handling, and they searched for the solution in their own matchless stock of racing experience. The Alfetta had met this same requirement, the need to keep the weight on the front and rear wheels approximately the same, by shifting the clutch and the gearbox from the front of the car to the rear. From the point of view of a production car, the extra advantage this had over the alternative solution of mounting the engine in the centre of the car was that it made no intrusion into the passenger or luggage space.

It was also the original Alfetta that provided the inspiration for the suspension system used at the rear of the car. When the problems of the simple swing-axle independent suspension had emerged during the 1950s, the Grand Prix cars had changed to de Dion axles, an arrangement that allows the rear wheels to move up and down independently, but with several important advantages. The wheels are always kept upright, without the camber changes inseparable from swing axles, and the unsprung weight is reduced to that of the simple tube that links the two wheels together. Alfa used a similar system on the new production car, with the addition of extra links to prevent the suspension moving sideways under cornering loads. The clutch, gearbox and differential were also linked in a single light, compact, alloy package together with the inboard rear disc brakes, and the whole mounted on the chassis to reduce the unsprung weight to the minimum.

All these changes were incorporated initially in a new body shape, with the 1.8-litre version of the twin-cam four inherited from the 1750 models. This was an entirely new Alfa saloon, which made its first appearance in May 1972: and in view of its pedigree, what better name for it than the Alfetta?

At first, the Alfetta co-existed with the 1750 and 2000 models, until new variants extended the single model into a range in its own right. Although it would eventually play its part in the company's motor sport endeavours, just as its illustrious predecessor had done, for the moment those efforts were being made in other areas.

Racing through the back door
The introduction of the beautiful Bertone Sprint Speciale in 1957 and a less exotic but equally purposeful opposite number from Carozzeria Zagato, the Giulietta SZ (for Sprint Zagato), in 1960 was to prove important for Alfa's sporting prestige. The latter was as light, as powerful and as fast as the SS, but it was aimed fairly and squarely at racing and, in the hands of private owners, it kept the Alfa name on the

ABOVE *The Alfetta name lives again in a range of production models for the 1970s and '80s. In fact the design shared several features with its racing car namesake, including de Dion rear suspension and a rear-mounted clutch, gearbox and differential unit.*

winners' lists until an even more ambitious car was ready. This was designed by the factory, but again Zagato was involved as a body-builder, and once more the basis of the new project was a production car: in this case the new Giulia design, which at the time (1959–60) was still under development.

It was, however, a radical redesign which only used the production model as a jumping-off point. The new car was built around a light and compact spaceframe made up of a closely meshed framework of small-bore tubes, covered with panelling which produced a body shape that was both elegant and efficient in cutting drag to the minimum. The rigid-axle rear suspension inherited from the 1900 and the Giulietta, which was to be used on the production Giulia, was here replaced by an independent version employing single wishbones, coil springs and upper transverse radius arms. The engine was initially the 112 bhp unit as used in the Giulia version of the SS and SZ, but the new car was so light – 650 kg (1430 lb) ready for the track – that it was capable of 217 km/h (135 mph), with circuit-car responses in roadholding and acceleration. The car was designated the Giulia TZ (for Tubolare Zagato), but was known universally as the Tubolare.

Unfortunately, there had been problems in the TZ's development, mainly because, in order to see the rest of the Giulia range safely launched, the people involved in it had to divert their attentions to the production-car priorities. The company therefore formed a completely new organization to develop and race the TZ and its eventual successors: this was called Autodelta, and was led by an ex-Alfa, ex-Ferrari, ex-ATS engineer called Carlo Chiti. From the beginning the results were encouraging. By the time the team entered its first proper racing season, in 1964, the five years of development that had gone into the car were soon to pay off, with class wins in many of the classic long-distance races, like Le Mans, the Targa Florio, the Sebring 12 Hours, and the Nürburgring 1000 Kilometres. In 1965, a lower, lighter version with a glass-fibre body called the TZ2 was to repeat many of these successes for a second season. By this time, however, there had been detail changes in the rules, under which a racing saloon more closely based on the production Giulia would make a better competitor in touring-car events.

ABOVE *Autodelta contested the postwar Targa Florios as keenly as Scuderia Ferrari had the prewar events. Here the Pinto/Todaro Giulia TZ2 is well on its way to a fourth place in the 1966 race. The TZ2 was a lower, lighter version of the earlier TZ.*

This was the reasoning that produced the Giulia GTA, introduced in 1965 and based on the GT Sprint. The A stood for *allegerita*, or 'lightened', thanks to a programme of weight reduction that included the replacement of steel body panelling with identically shaped components in aluminium. Various tuned versions of the Giulia engine were offered, but the team's own cars had a twin-plug version of the engine, with 10.5 to 1 compression ratio, which delivered 170 bhp at 7500 rpm and helped produce a top speed of 219 km/h (136 mph). Later, other variants were added, including the GTA-SA supercharged model, and the GTA Junior which used a wider-bore, shorter-stroke version of the Giulietta engine (78 × 67.5 mm instead of 74 × 75 mm, but with the same capacity of 1290 cc), delivering 165 bhp with fuel injection and the twin-plug head.

The GTAs were phenomenally successful within their chosen field: they won their classes in almost all the big races, which brought them three European Touring Car Championships in a row in the years 1966–8. In 1970, Autodelta applied the same treatment to the 1750 GTV, but to make it more competitive in the 2-litre class, the engine was bored out to 1985 cc, producing the 1750 GTAm, and it won another European Touring Car Championship for Alfa Romeo in its first racing season.

Alfa Romeo Giulia GTA
Years made 1965–9
No. made 500

ENGINE
Type	In-line
No. of cylinders	4
Bore/stroke mm	78 × 82
Displacement cc	1570
Valve operation	2 rows of inclined valves in roof of combustion chambers, directly actuated by twin ohc
Sparkplugs per cyl.	2
Compression ratio	9.7:1
Induction	2 horizontal twin-choke carburettors
BHP	115 at 6000 rpm

DRIVE TRAIN
Clutch	Single dry-plate
Transmission	5-speed manual gearbox, propeller shaft to rear axle

CHASSIS
Frame	Monocoque body–chassis unit
Weight	745 kg (1540 lb)
Wheelbase	2350 mm (7 ft 8½ in)
Track – front	1324 mm (4 ft 4 in)
Track – rear	1274 mm (4 ft 2¼ in)
Suspension – front	Independent, with coil springs and wishbones
Suspension – rear	Solid axle with coil springs and triangular locating bracket
Brakes	Servo-assisted discs
Tyre size	155HR × 15
Wheels	Light alloy disc

PERFORMANCE
Maximum speed	185 km/h (115 mph) +

The Giulia-based GTA took over most of the racing effort from the TZ2 in the later 1960s, after changes in the rules. Provided by R.W. Banks.

**Alfa Romeo 33/2
Sport Prototype (Daytona)**

Years made	1967–9
No. made	30

ENGINE

Type	90 degree V
No. of cylinders	8
Bore/stroke mm	78 × 52.2
Displacement cc	1995
Valve operation	2 rows of inclined valves in roof of combustion chambers, directly actuated by twin overhead camshafts for each cylinder bank
Sparkplugs per cyl.	2
Compression ratio	11:1
Induction	Fuel injection with twin electric pumps
BHP	270 at 9600 rpm

DRIVE TRAIN

Clutch	Single dry-plate,
Transmission	6-speed manual

CHASSIS

Frame	Large-diameter tubes welded in light alloy
Weight	580 kg (1276 lb)
Wheelbase	2250 mm (7 ft 4½ in)
Track – front	1336 mm (4 ft 3½ in)
Track – rear	1445 mm (4 ft 9 in)
Suspension	Independent, with coil springs and transverse bars
Brakes	Discs on all 4 wheels, actuated by twin hydraulic circuits
Tyre size – front	4.75 × 13
Tyre size – rear	6.00 × 13
Wheels	Light-alloy disc

PERFORMANCE

Maximum speed	298 km/h (186 mph)

The 33 Daytona on the banking at Monza. LOWER INSET *The 33 of Galli and Giunti on its way to second place in the 1968 Targa Florio.*

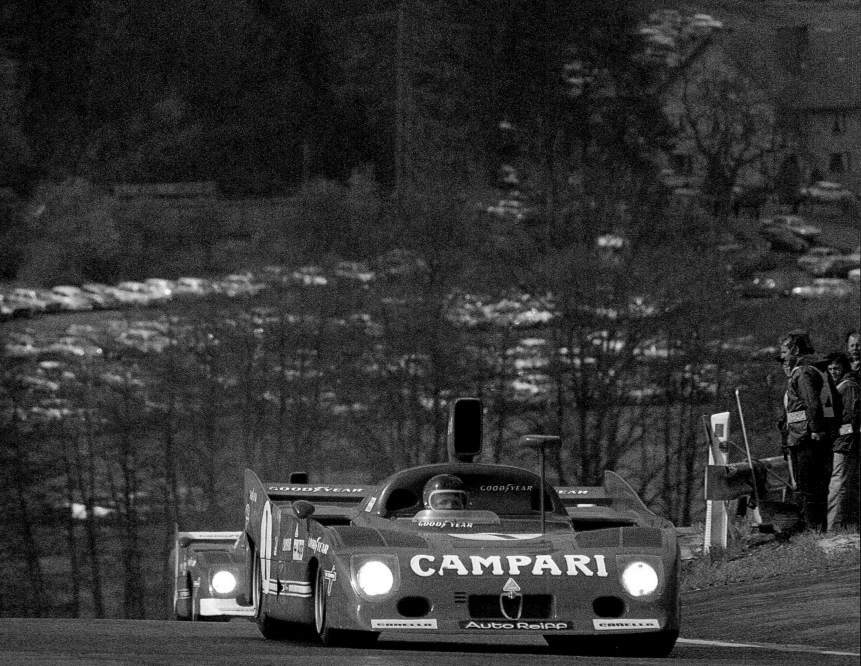

ABOVE *The Alfa Romeo Montreal was based on a Bertone-designed show car produced for the 1967 Expo at Montreal in Canada; almost 4000 of the production version were sold. Provided by The Patrick Collection.*

LEFT *In the 1975 season Alfa Romeo won yet another World Championship – this time for prototype racing – with the 33. Here Jacky Ickx heads for a second place in the 1975 Spa 1000 km: the winner was another 33.* INSET *the 3-litre 33SC12 won Alfa the Sports Car Championship in 1977; this is Merzario's car in the Dijon 500 km.*

The Tipo 33 project

By now, however, Autodelta and Alfa Romeo had become involved in a much bigger racing programme altogether with the T33 sports proto-type, which had been introduced in 1967. This had no links with any production Alfa at all, although the new V8 engine that powered the car had similarities with a design Chiti had produced for ATS some years before. The two cylinder banks were set at right angles to one another, and each one had the old Alfa formula of hemispherical combustion chambers with twin rows of inclined valves and twin overhead cam-shafts. In its original 1995 cc form it delivered 270 bhp and it was fitted, together with its six-speed gearbox, into the rear of a new racing chassis. This was made up of three large diameter tubes lined with rubber fuel tanks and arranged in an asymmetrical 'H' with light alloy castings at the ends of the 'H' to provide mounting points for the engine, transmission and suspension at the rear, and the steering, pedals and suspension at the front. Clothed in glass-fibre bodywork, the 33/2, as this version of the car was designated, looked splendidly promising, although its first year of competition was dogged by problems, mainly because of suspension failures. In 1968, however, the cars took first and second places in their class at the Daytona 24 Hours and consequently this version was named the Daytona in honour of that victory. They went on to win the first three places in their class at Le Mans in the same season, and were replaced the following year (1969) by the 33/3, which used a box-section chassis welded up from steel sheet, reinforced with titanium, and was powered by a 3-litre version of the V8 engine with four valves per cylinder and delivering 400 bhp. It had open glass-fibre bodywork on top. But to begin with the new cars proved dauntingly unreliable: only after patient development work did they succeed in winning second place in the 1972 Manufacturers'

World Championship series. Gaining that eagerly sought-after cham-pionship victory was to take a further three years, and yet another version of the car, the 33TT12, which not only reverted to tubular spaceframe construction (the 'TT' stood for *telaio tubolare*, 'tubular frame'), but also used a 3-litre flat-12 engine with twin overhead camshafts for each bank of cylinders, four valves and an output of 500 bhp. The 1975 victory was not the end of the 33 story, for two years later a sports version, the 33SC12, won the 1977 Sports Car Cham-pionship.

As we have seen, the 33 project was unusual in that it owed virtually nothing to any production Alfa: in fact, in a reversal of the usual progression, a production version of the racing car was made in small numbers during much of the 1970s. This owed its origins to the 1967 Montreal Expo, for which Bertone had produced an elegant coupé design based on Alfa Romeo components. Two years later, Alfa turned out a production version of the car, which had a roadgoing variant of the 90 degree V8 used in the 33, but with a capacity of 2593 cc and delivering 200 bhp. Unlike the mid-engined racer, the Montreal (as the new car was called) had the engine mounted at the front, driving the rear wheels through a five-speed gearbox. The unit was fitted with electronic ignition and fuel injection, and the car's top speed was more than 220 km/h (137 mph). Although it sold for twice the price of a 2000 GTV, and at first it was available to special order only, it proved immensely popular. Between 1970 and 1977, almost four thousand were sold: in terms of the strictly limited production run, it was one of the most successful of all the larger postwar Alfas.

With successes like these to crown the company's efforts during the 1970s, Alfa had a great deal to feel happy about. Yet there were problems to be faced which in many ways were to prove as challenging as any the company had met in its earlier history. Government directives would involve them in a costly and complex scheme to produce a radically new design of low-cost Alfa in the south of Italy, using a largely unskilled workforce in a completely new factory. Costs were rising, and income falling, at a time when even the racing challenges would prove more and more difficult to meet successfully. The later 1970s were to prove to be demanding years for Alfa Romeo, yet once again the company would have a chance to show that its extraordinary talent for survival had not diminished with the passing of the years.

The Present
and the Future

By 1975, when the 33 had won the championship, the pattern of the Alfa range of the mid-1980s had largely been set. The biggest change occurred in 1972 with the introduction of an Alfa based on a completely different philosophy, one that owed more to government intervention than marketing possibilities. This was the Alfasud ('Alfa South'), which was produced by a new design team working under Rudolf Hruska, and was to be built in a new factory on the site of one of Alfa's wartime aero engine plants in the south of Italy, at Pomigliano d'Arco near Naples, in an area of high unemployment. (Hruska was an Austrian engineer who had worked on the original Volkswagen project with Professor Ferdinand Porsche, and had been involved with the Cisitalia racing car scheme before joining Alfa in 1952.) The Alfasud itself was intended to broaden the range and to enter a new and important segment of the market; and in due course it would replace some of the smaller models. However, the new Alfasud really owed little to the earlier Giuliettas and Giulias in its basic engineering layout.

As was logical for an engineer who had started his career with Porsche and VW, it had a flat-4 engine, although in the case of the Alfasud it was mounted at the front of the car, where it allowed a low bonnet line for good visibility in a compact body that owed nothing in its styling to any other Alfa model. For all that, the Alfasud still had the feel and character of a true Alfa.

The design followed a radically different train of thought from the rest of the range. The water-cooled engine was fitted with overhead valves mounted in the roof of the combustion chambers – this at least followed Alfa's gospel – but in this case they were set in a single row and actuated by a single camshaft for each pair of cylinders. The engine was linked to a four-speed gearbox but, for the first time in any Alfa, the power unit drove the front wheels rather than the rear. The suspension, too, was different from the existing models: MacPherson struts were used at the front, and a rigid axle carried on coil springs and trailing arms at the rear.

Hruska's team of engineers went to considerable lengths to reduce weight as much as possible, producing a body which provided room for four people but with great inherent stiffness in the deep box sections at front and rear. With an engine of only 80 mm bore and 59 mm stroke, with a capacity of 1186 cc and a power output of 63 bhp, the body weight of a mere 830 kg (1830 lb) allowed a surprisingly lively performance with a maximum speed of more than 150 km/h (93 mph) and handling that was every bit as good as Alfa customers had come to expect from longer-established models.

The original Alfasud, despite its simple design philosophy, had instant appeal among customers who hitherto could not have afforded an Alfa Romeo – a new one at least. But following the typical progression from pedestrian (or relatively pedestrian) newcomer to more sporting derivatives, which had continued throughout the company's history, a high-performance version was brought out just over a year after production began. In the autumn of 1973 the Alfasud TI made its appearance, with compression raised from 8.8:1 to 9:1, and power up to 68 bhp which, with a five-speed gearbox and a neat, two-door body lighter than its predecessor by a useful 20 kg (44 lb), produced a genuine 160 km/h (100 mph) top speed. This was even better news for the enthusiasts, and a year later the original version was available with a five-speed gearbox as an option – the Alfasud 5m.

But as the popularity of the car increased, and other options with larger engines were added to the range, it became all too clear Alfa was having problems in turning out enough cars to meet the demand. Nevertheless, the range was augmented in 1976, with the addition of a completely new model to the line-up, in the form of the Alfasud Sprint. This had a lower and sleeker body, with a larger version of the flat-4 engine. It had the same 80 mm bore as the original, but the stroke was lengthened from 59 mm to 64 mm, enlarging the capacity from 1186 to 1286 cc, and increasing the power to 87 bhp. The top speed was now 165 km/h (103 mph), and even this was improved on in 1979 by the Sprint Veloces. The name Alfasud no longer appeared on these

PREVIOUS PAGES *One of Alfa's shapes for the 1980s. With its wedge-shaped lines the Alfa 33 Gold Cloverleaf represents a successor to the deservedly popular Alfasud and inherits its philosophy of a flat-4 engine driving the front wheels. Although in direct opposition to so much of the company's tradition, both cars possess the characteristic Alfa style.*

LEFT *The Alfasud was intended as a smaller, cheaper Alfa, but certain aspects were thoroughly in keeping with Alfa tradition: in particular, the introduction of a faster TI version, like this 1982 Alfasud 1.5TI. Provided by Vernon Thompson.*

RIGHT *Ever since the earliest days, the Alfa range has always contained at least one open two-seater, and this – the 2000 Spider – survives in today's production line-up. Apart from successive increases in engine size, producing first the 1750 Spider and then the 2000, and the chopping off of the tail, the chassis is still that of the Duetto (the 1600 Spider) of 1966. Provided by Ron W. Callard.*

Alfa Romeo Sprint 1.5 Green Cloverleaf

Years made 1983 to date
No. made Still in production

ENGINE		CHASSIS	
Type	Horizontally opposed	**Frame**	Monocoque body–chassis unit
No. of cylinders	4	**Weight**	915 kg (2013 lb)
Bore/stroke mm	84 × 67.2	**Wheelbase**	2455 mm (8 ft 1 in)
Displacement cc	1490	**Track – front**	1397 mm (4 ft 7 in)
Valve operation	Single row of valves in roof of combustion chamber, directly actuated by single overhead camshaft in each bank of cylinders	**Track – rear**	1364 mm (4 ft 6 in)
		Suspension – front	Independent, with MacPherson struts and anti-roll bar
Sparkplugs per cyl.	1	**Suspension – rear**	Rigid axle, with coil springs, Panhard rod and Watts linkage
Compression ratio	9:1		
Induction	2 twin-choke down-draught carburettors	**Brakes**	Servo-assisted disc brakes on all 4 wheels, dual hydraulic circuits
BHP	105 at 6000 rpm	**Tyre size**	TRX 190/55 HR 340
		Wheels	Alloy disc
DRIVE TRAIN			
Clutch	Single dry plate, hydraulically operated	**PERFORMANCE**	
Transmission	5-speed manual gearbox, driving front wheels	**Maximum speed**	185 km/h (115 mph)

ABOVE *The most striking variation on the Alfasud theme, and one that outlived its parent design, was the sleek and handsome Sprint. The bodywork was lowered and lightened to produce a much more purposeful shape, and this was fitted with engines of progressively larger sizes and power outputs. This represents the top of the current range: the Alfa Romeo Sprint 1.5 Green Cloverleaf. In this form the Alfasud engine displaces 1490cc and produces 105 bhp. Since the demise of the orthodox Alfasud range, the name has been dropped from the car's official designation.*

Alfa Rome Giulietta 2.0
Years made 1980 to date
No. made Still in production

ENGINE		CHASSIS	
Type	In-line	**Frame**	Monocoque body–chassis unit
No. of cylinders	4		
Bore/stroke mm	84 × 88.5	**Weight**	1100 kg (2425 lb)
Displacement cc	1962	**Wheelbase**	2510 mm (8 ft 3 in)
Valve operation	2 rows of inclined valves in roof of combustion chambers, actuated directly by twin overhead camshafts	**Track – front**	1360 mm (4 ft 5½ in)
		Track – rear	1350 mm (4 ft 5 in)
		Suspension – front	Independent, with torsion bars and double wishbones
Sparkplugs per cyl.	1	**Suspension – rear**	Independent, with de Dion tube, coil springs and Watts linkage
Compression ratio	9:1		
Induction	2 horizontal twin-choke carburettors	**Brakes**	Servo-assisted discs operated by twin hydraulic circuits
BHP	130 at 5400 rpm		
DRIVE TRAIN		**Tyre size**	185/65 HR 14
Clutch	Single dry-plate, hydraulically operated	**Wheels**	Pressed-steel disc
Transmission	5-speed manual gearbox, mounted at rear	**PERFORMANCE**	
		Maximum speed	185 km/h (115 mph)

variants, in preparation for phasing out the Alfasud saloons altogether. The idea that the Alfasud operation should have a separate identity was now less essential for political reasons, and Alfa itself felt happier to emphasize the unity between the company's different operations by bringing them together under the Alfa Romeo designation instead.

The Sprint Veloces offered two more versions of the flat-4 engine. The 1.3 had a longer-stroke 67.2 mm, 1350 cc unit delivering 86 bhp and giving a top speed of more than 170 km/h (106 mph); the 1.5 had a wider-bore 84 × 67.2 mm, 1490 cc, 95 bhp version with maximum speed in excess of 175 km/h (109 mph). Most powerful of all was to be the 105 bhp version of the larger engine which powered the 1983 Sprint 1.5 Quadrifoglio Verde (Green Cloverleaf) to produce a top speed of 180 km/h (112 mph). This engine was also used in the Green Cloverleaf variant of the Alfasud TI saloon.

Recent production Alfas

From this point on, the Alfa story becomes more complex still, with more models, more engines and more permutations of the two. The original Alfetta saloon had been joined by a Giugiaro-styled coupé, the Alfetta GT, in 1973, which used the 1.8-litre version of the twin-cam engine as employed in the 1750 models. Later, both the saloon and the coupé also emerged with 1.6- and 2-litre engines, inherited from the Giulias and the 2000 models respectively. The saloons were outwardly identical, apart from details like headlamps, and of course embellishments identifying them as the Alfetta 1.8 and the Alfetta 2000. In the case of the coupés, the two versions were named the GT 1.6 and the GTV 2000 respectively. Both had the elegant but unfamiliar (in terms of earlier GTV shapes) Giugiaro design, built around the Alfetta package with torsion bar front suspension, de Dion axle at the rear, front engine and clutch, gearbox and differential at the rear of the car, and disc brakes all round. These were introduced in the mid-1970s, and in the mid-1980s the GTV still formed part of the current range.

If the Alfettas, like the 1750s, owed their names to other cars in the company's past, the next group of models derived their names from a more recent precursor still: the Giulietta. In this case, the new

Giulietta was also based on the Alfetta mechanicals and the same chassis, although with a body much more square cut, and slightly shorter, lower and wider, in a wedge-shaped configuration ending in a high boot. The original models appeared with a choice of two engines: the 1570 cc as used in the Giulia range, and a new, smaller version of the twin-cam four-cylinder unit with a bore of 80 mm and a stroke of 67.5 mm, producing a capacity of 1357 cc and a power output of 95 bhp. With this engine, the Giulietta had a top speed of 165 km/h (103 mph); with the large unit it was capable of 175 km/h (109 mph). Later, the Giulietta became available with the 1.8-litre engine originally developed for the 1750 range, and eventually the 2-litre 1962 cc unit as developed for the 2000 models, and used subsequently for the Alfetta 2000 and the 2000 GTV. In this form, the Giulietta 2.0 has a maximum speed of 185 km/h (115 mph).

This far, the recent development story of production Alfas has tended to centre on new body shapes which used existing engines. In 1980, however, a modified Alfetta saloon bodyshell was fitted with a totally new, 88 × 63 mm, 2492 cc, 160 bhp V6 power unit and introduced as the flagship of the range: the Alfa 6. This was the first six-cylinder Alfa for more than a decade, and the company hopes it will win the popularity that has seemed to elude large and luxurious Alfas, when compared with their smaller and sportier brethren. Certainly, the shape of the car seems familiar enough, and the smoothness and willingness of the engine have given the 6 a high reputation, even among those enthusiasts accustomed to the apparently immortal four-cylinder unit.

The Alfa 6 is outshone by its fuel-injected stablemate, the GTV6, which uses the same engine in the GTV body, a formula that produces a top speed of 205 km/h (127 mph) – although the saloon can manage a creditable 197 km/h (122 mph) in its own right. These are the present-day equivalents of the 2600 saloons and coupés of the 1960s, Alfas that can provide the verve and performance enthusiasts expect in larger and more luxurious packages than the bulk of the range – but only time will tell whether these versions will sell in large enough quantities to be commercially viable.

LEFT *Alfa has made a deliberate point of naming several new models after popular Alfas of the past, as a way of reminding buyers of the company's illustrious history. First the 1750, then the Alfetta – and then the Giulietta. In this case a neatly styled, wedge-shaped saloon which has been fitted with a succession of alternative engines, and uses a modified version of the transmission, suspension and running gear of the Alfettas. These pictures show the current top-of-the-range Giulietta 2.0*

RIGHT *Successor to the 2600 series of big Alfas, the Alfa 6 uses the basic mechanical layout of the Alfetta, while the body style has a more than passing resemblance to that of the standard Alfetta saloon. The engine, however, is quite different: a 2.5-litre V6, intended to endow the car with the smoothness and flexibility that a car aimed at this part of the market needs. This concept has tended to be rather at odds with the spirit and performance of the company's sportier and more popular cars.*

In Grand Prix racing again

The other link with the past that has persisted through the 1970s and '80s has been Alfa's continuing involvement with Grand Prix racing. This began as far back as 1970, when the McLaren team elected to use the Alfa Romeo 3-litre V8 as developed for the 33 racing programme. However, the engine's lack of power, compared with its GP opponents, brought the collaboration to an end in 1971, the year in which the March team chose to use an Alfa unit. The Alfa-engined car only appeared in two events: on one occasion it crashed and on the other, the engine blew itself up.

More promising altogether was the Alfa Romeo flat-12, which was to give the 33s their 1975 World Championship. In 1975, the company signed an agreement to supply engines to the Brabham team for the BT45 Formula One car. These 3-litre engines were worked on by Autodelta to reduce the weight as much as possible (the extra weight and lack of low-speed torque had plagued the V8 in its Grand Prix form), and to raise the power to more than 520 bhp; but ultimately the whole exercise proved to be as frustrating as chasing the German cars had been during the 1930s.

In the end, the company took the only logical step remaining to it: Alfa re-entered Grand Prix racing in 1979 with a car of its own, for the first time since 1951. There was a great deal of lost ground to be made up; and there was now no question of diverting company brainpower, as

BELOW *The original Alfetta GT had a 1.8 version of the twin-cam engine; later came a 1.6 GT and a 2-litre, designated the GTV. Finally a fuel-injected version of the 2.6-litre V6 was fitted to the car to produce the quickest of the range, the current GTV6.*

LEFT *A coupé version of the Alfetta had bodywork designed by Giugiaro. This was the Alfetta GT, which was pressed into sporting service in the fine old tradition. Alfetta GTs, like this one in the San Remo Rally, won Alfa two European Championships.*

Alfa Romeo GTV6

Years made	1981 to date
No. made	Still in production

ENGINE

Type	60 degree V
No. of cylinders	6
Bore/stroke mm	88 × 68.3
Displacement cc	2492
Valve operation	2 rows of inclined valves in roof of combustion chambers, actuated by one overhead camshaft per cylinder bank
Sparkplugs per cyl.	1
Compression ratio	9:1
Induction	Fuel injection
BHP	160 at 5600 rpm

DRIVE TRAIN

Clutch	Dual dry-plates hydraulically operated
Transmission	5-speed manual gearbox

CHASSIS

Frame	Monocoque body–chassis unit
Weight	1210 kg (2668 lb)
Wheelbase	2400 mm (7 ft 10 in)
Track – front	1366 mm (4 ft 6 in)
Track – rear	1358 mm (4 ft 5½ in)
Suspension – front	Independent, with torsion bars and double wishbones
Suspension – rear	Independent, with de Dion tube, coil springs and Watts linkage
Brakes	Servo-assisted discs on all four wheels, double hydraulic circuits
Tyre size	195/60 HR 15
Wheels	Alloy disc

PERFORMANCE

Maximum speed	205 km/h (127 mph)

FAR LEFT *The 'Alfa Romeo' name on the nose of this racing car tells the whole story. This is the 1976 Formula One Brabham, which used the first Alfa Grand Prix engine for a quarter of a century: the 3-litre flat-12.*

ABOVE *Later Alfa was to re-enter Grand Prix racing with its own cars as well as power units. Here is Andrea de Cesaris' Alfa Romeo 183T at the 1983 Monaco GP.*

LEFT *Patrese's 1984 F1 Alfa at the British Grand Prix. So far results have been disappointing, but new engines promise better prospects for the future.*

in the old days, to make good this deficiency. In other words, although the Alfa GP car carried the Alfa name, the size of the team, and its resources, were really ascribable to Autodelta rather than the parent company. The Formula One car has so far not been all that successful, although it did achieve a creditable third place in the Italian Grand Prix at Monza in 1984.

On the other hand, Alfa Romeo itself points to likely changes in GP racing that may well bring some return on its efforts. Indeed, Grand Prix racing undergoes constant technological change, and new requirements are emerging, notably in the fields of turbocharged engines and highly sophisticated aerodynamics to offset the problems created by some fundamental alterations to the rules. These regulations had previously allowed the use of sliding side skirts and other extreme aids to chassis performance. Along with other participants in this form of motor racing, Alfa Romeo was to discover that reliability, which previously had been at a generally quite high level, would be an increasingly significant factor in achieving success. The company's last normally aspirated racing engine, a V12, was to prove on occasions impressively fast, but the works cars and those of other teams

that used the engine were never to achieve actual race-winning performance, and in due course the V12 was to be put back on the shelf to make way for a turbocharged V8. This, too, was to prove very powerful and effective on some circuits, but Alfa's performance was repeatedly to be harmed by the thirstiness of this engine, which on several occasions failed to last the full race, once stringent fuel tankage limits had been introduced.

However, it was hoped that this frustrating period, which again inhibited the Alfa Romeo team from achieving outright race victories, would be ended by the development and scheduled appearance in 1985 of another new turbocharged unit: the first four-cylinder Alfa Romeo Grand Prix engine since 1914.

Whichever way you look at Alfa's Formula One programme – as an optimist or as a pessimist – there is little doubt that the decisions resulting from the 1985 season are likely to be of long-term significance. Another series of disappointments might bring final withdrawal much closer, while success with the new engine may well bring a much more vigorous, and ultimately victorious, effort in this highest class of motor racing.

ABOVE *Latest in the Alfetta front-engined, rear-clutch-and-gearbox stable is the Alfa 90, which uses the same V6 engine as introduced on the Alfa 6, but in a lower, leaner Bertone body which sets out to provide a more up-to-date package for the upmarket Alfa saloon. It is aimed at competitors like the Mercedes-Benz 190.*

A Japanese connection

We must now look at the new generation of Alfa Romeos to take the company, and its customers, forward into the 1990s. Just as British Leyland went into partnership with the Japanese company Honda to produce cars like the Triumph Acclaim and, later, the Rover 213, Alfa Romeo entered into a similar arrangement with Nissan to produce an Italian-Japanese hybrid called the Arna, to make use of Alfa's spare engine manufacturing capacity. The reasoning was this: the Alfasud project was showing its age, with falling sales resulting from increased competition in this market segment. This meant spare production capacity, and a large workforce with too few cars to make. One solution was the new model designed as an Alfasud replacement, the Alfa 33, which used the chassis and mechanicals of the latest versions of that range. It featured a new body with a strong family resemblance to the Giulietta, and a completely new production line with a high proportion of robot assembly sections, together with new painting and finishing systems. A neat four-door saloon, it became available with a choice of two four-cylinder engines: 1.3 and 1.5 litres. With power at around 80 to 85 bhp, both versions were capable of more than 160 km/h (100 mph), with 0–60 mph figures of 11 seconds.

The 33 on its own could not, however, keep the whole production capacity occupied; yet developing and producing the components for the more up-market versions of the 33 that were on the way (the Gold Cloverleaf and Green Cloverleaf variants which were to use the more powerful 1.5-litre flat-4 engines) meant more expense and smaller volumes. So the solution adopted was to let the 33 find its own production level, and to use the spare capacity for the Arna. Alfa produced the mechanical parts for this car, which were then assembled into a body designed and developed in Japan but actually manufactured in Italy. This meant low costs and high volume, and a car that was produced under the Alfa name as the Arna in Italy, but would be called the Nissan Cherry Europe in some other countries.

Future challenges — and solutions

The result, from Alfa's point of view, has been very successful. The Arna was carefully and effectively distanced from Alfa's own models at first, but the company is now making it more of an Alfa, to tie it in more closely with the rest of the range. The 33 is proving to be extremely attractive to Alfa buyers as a worthy successor to the deservedly popular Alfasud, and the Naples operation in the south has been turned from a damaging loss into a successful and profitable project in its own right.

And what of the future? Alfa's productivity has been increased by more than 35 per cent overall, and the future promises to be an interesting one. First on the list of new introductions is the Alfa 90, a sports saloon with the Alfetta chassis, the V6 engine and a new Bertone body design – leaner and more compact than the Alfa 6 and aimed at

competitors like the Mercedes-Benz 190. The Alfa 90 will represent the upper end of the market, with the 33 at the lower end, and a series of sporty new models progressively making their appearance in between. First to appear, in 1985, will probably be a high-power four-door saloon. Another will be the Type 164, developed jointly with Lancia and Fiat to use a common chassis, gearbox and suspension. The 164 will be an even more prestigious model in the Alfa range. It will be a car to look forward to.

Other new models later on in the pipeline are likely to make use of different versions of one of Alfa's more intriguing projects, the modular engine. This is a unit that would enable half the engine's cylinders to shut down when the engine is running on light throttle openings. Alfa

BELOW *The shape of things to come? Alfa is not alone in its collaboration with a big Japanese company (in this case Nissan) to produce a successful seller. This is the Arna, which uses Alfa mechanical parts in a body designed in Japan and produced in Italy. Nissan sells the car as the Cherry Europe.*

took eight years to develop its own sophisticated electronic engine control system, CEM, which combined fuel injection and ignition timing in a very refined and responsive way – and at a time when the Grand Prix engine was sadly blighted by lack of an efficient electronic ignition system!

This CEM system has now been taken a stage further. By the use of microprocessor circuitry, not only can the throttle opening determine how many cylinders in an engine are actually working, but the system also ensures that that work is shared evenly between the cylinders to prevent some of them cooling down. The treatment has already been applied to the flat-4 in a prototype called the SVAR, and to the twin-cam four unit in a fleet of Milan taxis, where fuel economy has increased by 25 per cent.

With ideas like these on the way, improvements in quality and productivity, new models and new designs, it seems that Alfa's future may prove to be as successful, and as fascinating, as its past. For that to be the case, the company has a great deal to live up to – but it also has a great deal to inspire it.

Index

Figures in *italics* refer to captions to illustrations.

Acknowledgements

The publishers wish to thank the following organizations and individuals for their kind permission to reproduce the photographs in this book;
Alfa Romeo SpA, Italy 8, 10 below, 12-13, 16 below, 17 above right, 21, 23 above, 24 left, 35 below, 39, 42, 45 above, 46, 56 above, 60, 66 inset, 73, 75 inset; Geoffrey Goddard 62, 65 below; Chris Harvey 77 below; Cyril Posthumus 32 left; Nigel Snowdon and Associates 66, 76, 77 above.

All other photographs specially taken by Ian Dawson.

In addition, the publishers would like to thank the following: Cornelis Verweij, Raimondo Corsi di Turri and Domenico Magro from Alfa Romeo SpA in Italy; N. Barrington Needham and Janet Betham of Alfa Romeo (Great Britain) Ltd; Angela Cherrett of the Alfa Romeo Section (VSCC Ltd); and Michael Lindsay of the Alfa Romeo Owners' Club. The publishers would also like to thank Alfa Romeo SpA for giving them permission to photograph the cars in the Alfa Romeo Museum in Arese. Finally, thanks are due to the owners or custodians of the other cars who kindly allowed their vehicles to be photographed.